The Bastard Regiment

Abraham Norton

Table of Contents

Macon County, North Carolina in the American Civil War

Volume I

Company B and I, 39th North Carolina: The Bastard Regiment

Authored By: Abraham F.C. Norton

Chapter 1

In 7 sentences. I understand that it is unlikely that I will garner a great deal of attention from a large percentage of the population in today's world, as this story is too descriptive to fit in 7 sentences. But my goal is not to captivate the world with many details, but if that's what you want and if you are willing to, you will certainly find plenty of further information past Chapter 1. The deal with 7 sentences is if I will not be able to captivate your attention long, I want to keep at least the Macon County men that served in the 39th North Carolina alive and remembered for as many generations as possible. Below is my best shot at getting their legacy into seven sentences so that if you do not read my whole book, you'll at least know they existed.

Companies B and I were first raised for confederate service on 19th October 1861 and 25th March 1862. Approximately 270 Macon County men made up those two companies. They became part of the 39th Regiment of North Carolina Troops. They fought in around 17 battles in Tennessee, Georgia, Alabama, and Mississippi. The Macon County men were there for it all, and their exploits at The Battle of Chickamauga led them to be part of "The Star Brigade" of Chickamauga. Macon County lost a total of 84 men that served in the 39th North Carolina, which meant that 31.11% of the Macon County men never made it home, a little less than 1/3. Macon County served with distinction and honor in all their engagements. The 39th was surrendered, and 25 Macon County men over a month General Robert E. Lee's surrender.

There are 7 sentences. If you are still with me, I am forever grateful that you would like to know more details about what made Company B and I of the 39th North Carolina, such a special group of men. I first learned that I had a confederate ancestor via my maternal grandmother when I was very young. I do not know how young, but it was definitely prior to 2nd grade. My grandmother, like myself, was always highly fascinated by military history. She was excited to tell me about all our families that had occupied the American ranks of every major American War. She was married to a World War II Veteran, and at the time, she was filling my head too with military history. My cousin Heath (her grandson) was serving as a military policeman. He, of course, was the son of a Vietnam Infantry Veteran. Military service was a big deal in our family.

I had lots of questions and not a lot of capacity to understand what war really was. I was concerned with who the good guys and bad guys were. As I listened to various relatives in various wars, I asked obvious questions like, "Who were the bad guys, grandma?" The answers were easy, the Germans, the Koreans, the

Japanese, the Cubans, the British, and the list of bad guys were easy to list off. Then I asked about Grandpa Beasley Beasley and his barefooted, half-naked walk home from prison in Chicago when the war was over, "Who were those those bad guys, grandma?"

The answer did not come as quickly. She said, "well, we were the bad guys, Abraham." I found myself confused. This led to a long line of further conversations that culminated in one thing that my grandma, a very proud Southerner was already aware that the very foundations of the Southern cause were unjust. As you read this, you are starting to think maybe I will go on a long rant about the injustice of slavery and anger southerners everywhere. I am not. Let me make this very clear; slavery is awful, it's terrible, and what African Americans endured in America was nothing short of horrifying. African Americans nor anyone in the world deserved that sort of treatment. It happened, and it was ONE of the most significant determining factors in the war. It is ignorant to say that the Civil War had nothing to do with slavery, but it's also ignorant to say that every soldier was either fighting for or against slavery. That was not the case at all.

At the onset of the war, Abraham Lincoln felt slavery was a constitutional right, and as you famously know, if he could have saved the Union without freeing a slave, he would have done it. Perhaps you do not buy into that, or you feel that his opinion changed as the war went on. I will buy that argument, but it means that when Lincoln invaded the South, it was not about slavery. Lincoln even proposed that once slavery was abolished that slaves in disposition would need to move back to Africa. If you still do not believe this, feel free to look it up and see for yourself. If slavery was so important to Lincoln, why did he allow the slave states of Kentucky, Missouri, Maryland, and Delaware to fight in the Union Army? Also, did you know that the year Lincoln was elected that there were 451,021 slaves in the North? Slaves were still inside of the Nation's Capital! In 1865, when the war ended, New Jersey released its last 16 slaves with the passage of the thirteenth amendment.

Perhaps you still think these are mere technicalities and Lincoln was just willing to accept slavery in states on the premise they helped with the war? Let me tell you, when Lincoln passed the Emancipation Proclamation, it did not include the Northern Slave States, isn't that peculiar? Does that not take away the point? Is it not also backwards to think that slavery is wrong but still buy slave sourced cotton for use in Northern factories? Slavery is terrible, but the more I've read into the issue of slavery, I find that it was not just a Southern sin; it was an American sin.

There has always been an extensive argument over whether African Americans served in the confederate army. Within the context of Macon County, North Carolina's Civil War experience, I have not found any African Americans that bore the confederate uniform for Macon County. I have seen several African American/Caucasian soldiers that did, though. There was only one man in the 39th North Carolina, but several others were within other Macon County companies. One thing, which is a historical fact, is that African American soldiers fought in the union ranks. The union, however, did not think enough of them to let them be officers or be a part of white units. They literally gave them unit designations which included the verbiage "Colored Troops."

If the South bore that sin alone, let's remember that the confederacy died in 1865. African Americans were not allowed to be in white units until 1948. Apparently, the South was the cause of American racism. Once the South was destroyed, it took the United States 83 years to integrate the armed services. Racism did not start with the Southern States, and it did not end with the Southern States. I could get into all the politics of 2021, but I think it is apparent that in the year 2021, in which I am writing Chapter 1, racism is very much alive. Some of the worst racial events of the past few years have been very far north of the Mason-Dixon Line, and the confederacy has been dead for 156 years now.

Maybe the confederacy was not the only problem back then. When Lincoln was done, the same officers that were apparently fighting to end slavery next turned their guns on Native Americans as Manifest Destiny continued in post-confederate America and went to work dominating the West Coast. If the Union sought to save slaves only, I guess they just did not feel the same way about Native Americans?

I hate to be political, but I know that nowadays, to even talk about the fighting men of the American Civil War, you must address its politics. The only problem with that is, the fighting men of any war are never so convenient that you can just paint them with one broad brush. If was in the War on Terror. I have heard all sorts of reasons for the war. Most of them are not why I served, and for every friend I made, I generally found another reason. I know of almost as many reasons as I knew people. To think that we can boil down the Civil War to one issue is a ridiculous sentiment. There were men connected to slavery in the 39th. The overwhelming majority had no connection to slavery whatsoever. However, it equates that they all fought for slavery or maintained themselves a rung higher than the slaves. Based on their writings back home and what they said, I do not buy that explanation at all. Many of the fighting men got wrapped up in it the same way I did, in the excitement of it all.

A massive issue of the Civil War was slavery. Another significant issue was money. Today our world is still driven by those two things. Various products that we buy today are stained in slave labor. I do not just mean the cheap labor around the world that is problematic. I do not just mean child labor. Many of our supply chains still have literal unpaid slavery in them. Why do you buy their products? I will not say names as I do not want my little book to deal with the big dogs, which is completely justifiable. But why do you support companies that use children at low rates? Why do you buy products that do not pay employees enough to live? Why do you buy products that literally have slave labor in their supply chains? There are some very large companies out there that are engaging in these practices. You support them with your money, but you have the audacity to judge people from over 150 years ago that did not have all the information of the world at their fingertips. You have it all, but you still support the very companies that engage in these activities. American has come a long way, but one thing still prevails the same way it did back then; if the money is right, good people will look the other way.

This story is about a misunderstood group of fighting men who fought for around 4 years as hard as possible for something. Something compelled them to leave their isolated County of North Carolina and march away to fight for something. Perhaps we do not understand what led many of the fighting men to feel they were fighting an invasion, like when their grandfathers had fought the American Revolution. They had an intense patriotism evident in their letters home, the newspapers of the day, and in their actions on the battlefield. This story is meant to focus on the men of Company B and Company I 39th North Carolina, but naturally, it lends itself to the entire history of the 39th North Carolina because everywhere that Company B and I went there, too was the rest of the 39th North Carolina.

This story is told by years of oral history, book research, internet research, and perhaps the best part is some of the stories are in their own words. I have the luck of having access to Captain Alfred Bell's firsthand accounts, Sergeant William Tippett, and then also 3 men in the regiment that were not from Macon County. We hear from Sergeant Major Theodore Davidson of Cherokee, Lieutenant John Davidson of Cherokee County, and Lieutenant Benjamin Cathey of Jackson County. Without their firsthand accounts, the story would lack a lot of its richest soldierly details.

This book is dedicated to all my confederate ancestors emphasizing on my most direct links in Pvt. Joseph Manson Beasley and Pvt. Andrew Jackson Stiles.

Without them, I would have never been inspired to tell the stories of the rest of the 39th. If they had not marched away from Macon County, these stories likely would have never been known by me. I also want to dedicate this book to my grandma Leneta Crisp. Without her, I would have never developed this passion. They wrote the story, and I am just here to share it with you.

Act I

Macon County's Company B and I's Conception into the 39th North Carolina

19th October 1862-31st July 1862

Chapter 2

The first company of Maconians in the 39th was raised at Franklin on 19th October 1861. The men of Company B have formed under their Dentist Captain Alfred Bell and their School Teacher 1st Lieutenant William T. Anderson. Their 2nd Lieutenant was a man named Joshua C. Bird, who was voted out when the battalion got organized as a regiment. The 2nd Lieutenant that replaced him was 2nd Lieutenant Thomas Roane. The 3rd Lt. was a laborer by the name of William A. Holbrook. Of the 4 men originally elected, Bell was from the town of Franklin, Anderson and Holbrook from the township of Tennessee Valley, and Bird hailed from the township of Cowee. None of the original officers of Company B was from households that owned slaves. However, I cannot withhold the fact that Captain Bell became a slave owner during the war.

Along with the four officers, Company B enlisted 68 men bringing the total company manpower to 72. Among that number, there was 1 enlisted man that came from a home that owned slaves. After the initial enlistment, at various points in the war, another 74 men enlisted in total. Of that 74, an additional 4 men came from a home that owned slaves. Considering Captain Bell as the company's 1 actual slave owner and 5 others who came from slave-owning homes, the demographic of Company B was 4.11% connected to the ownership of slaves. Anything over 0% is unacceptable, but over 95% of Company B and 97% of the original enlistees did not come from slave-owning households, and .007% of the company ever purchased a slave. One member of the regiment was a private by the name of John L. Guy. There has been a great deal of argument over the years about whether the confederacy had any African Americans in their ranks. John L. Guy was bi-racial. This does not change the context of slavery in any way but simply sheds light on the fact that a bi-racial man fought and died with the 39th North Carolina. He took a severe wound at Murfreesboro in his left leg. When he died on 15th February 1864, it was attributed to his left leg and wounding at Murfreesboro.

The company was ordered to Camp Patton, Asheville, North Carolina. It joined David Coleman's Battalion and was designated as Company B. Coleman's Battalion received official recognition, and David Coleman received the rank of Major on 10th December 1861. David Coleman was a 37-year-old attorney from Buncombe County. Coleman was well educated and was already a veteran. Coleman was unique in that he had served in the U.S. Navy abroad in Africa, The Middle East, and South America. He also served with the navy in The Mexican War, and his vessel took part in the naval bombardment at The Battle of Veracruz. Coleman also served two terms in the U.S. Senate and defeated North

Carolina's wartime Governor Zebulon Vance in the Senate Race of 1856, which secured his second term. In 1858, Vance defeated him for Congress. Coleman was the only candidate that ever beat Governor Vance in an election.

Coleman was firmly in favor of the secession at a very early stage. His doctrines were well received in his home county of Buncombe, but Coleman came near to being tarred and feather when he took his secession talk on the road to Madison County. The loyalties of the region were so divided in the mountains of North Carolina that in the Secessionist movement, even those for secession were not outspoken like Coleman was. As the war began, Coleman immediately volunteered to serve in the confederate army. His past naval experience made the confederate government originally slate him for naval service. The Confederate War Machine was slow in getting a navy up and going, and Northern Naval Superiority quickly had the Southern States efficiently blockaded. With this and his impatience to get to the field, Coleman headed to Asheville, intending to raise his own infantry regiment instead.

We do not have a lot of information on the activities of Company B between 19th October 1861 and the organization of Coleman's Battalion into a regiment. The first record we see of Company B's activities came on 10th January 1862 when Captain Bell wrote a letter home to his wife. Bell did not say anything really of interest other than talk of men that had deserted back to Macon County and trying to arrange to bring his wife and children to stay at one of the local houses near his camp. At the top of the letter, he referred to their camp as Camp Coleman. This was a move from Camp Patton, but this area was referred to as Reems Creek in the official records.

On 18th January 1862, Captain Bell wrote to his wife that he had been able to secure his men 100 overcoats, 100 caps and apparently had the means to get as much clothing at that time as he wanted. The men of Company B, as of January 1862, were well dressed and had such an ample supply that he was worried about loading the men down with clothing. Bell also had the means to clothe his officers and have them kepis made. For the rest of January 1862, several detachments of the 39th were used to find and bring deserters back to camp.

In early February, the men received a shipment for Raleigh, which included lamb rifles, haversacks, and knapsacks. The men heard all sorts of rumors about where they would be heading when they got active field orders, and Bell was hoping for Coastal North Carolina so he could eat oysters and fish. Then on 15th February 1862, 2 Companies were added to the battalion. With these companies' addition, the Battalion was reorganized as a Battalion of 7 Companies allowing Major Coleman to be promoted to Lieutenant Colonel Coleman on 16th

February 1862. These two additional companies were very small and were formed from a combination of men in Companies A and C. This move was likely made to simply create more companies so the battalion could be upgraded to a regiment.

Not long after this reconsolidation, another Company arrived from Cherokee County. It was designated as Company H. The battalion was then moved to Knoxville, Tennessee and received its first Brigade Assignment under General Danville Leadbetter. The battalion moved to Clinton, Tennessee, where they went into camp for the winter from Knoxville.

Chapter 3

Meanwhile, back in Franklin, Sheriff James Crawford was organizing Macon's second company destined for service in Coleman's Battalion. This company would become Company I of Coleman's Battalion. Crawford was 29-years-old and lived in the area of Macon known as the Tennessee Valley. He also left behind a 21-year-old wife named Virginia and a 2-year-old daughter named Ellen. Crawford's officers were 1st Lieutenant John Reid, 2nd Lieutenant William Pulaski Norton, 3rd Lieutenant Robert H. Smith. William P. Norton declined the appointment as 2nd Lieutenant, and the position was given to Robert H. Smith. A 3rd Lieutenant was not named until 30th April 1862, when 3rd Lieutenant Rufus Swain Siler was elected to the post.

I do not know much about what Lt. Smith was doing before the war other than he was 18-years-old. Lt. Reid was also from the Tennessee Valley with a wife named Salena and 3 children ranging in age from 5-9. Lt. Rufus Swain Siler was a 25-year-old from Cowee that as of 1860, was living in the home of his father, Jacob. His father, Jacob, owned 9 slaves. None of the other officers in Company I owned slaves, nor did they live in slave-owning households. In addition to 5 original officers, 1 of which declined the assignment, 90 men enlisted in the original company. Out of those 90 men, 5 men hailed from slave-owning households and 1 private named Pressley Norton. Pressley Norton hailed from the Tennessee Valley area and owned 2 slaves.

During the war, 29 additional men enlisted in Company I, and none of them were slave-owners or came from slave-owning households. With a total number served to be 124, Company I had 1 slave-owner and 6 men that came from slave-owning households. The company had around 5.65% of its ranks that hailed came from slave-owning households. As stated earlier, anything over 0% is too high, but over 94% of the men didn't come from Slave Owning Households. Of the 82 Slave Owning Households in Macon County before the War, Companies B and I had enlisted men from 9 of them. Macon County was home to 855 additional homes which did not own any slaves. There were 258 men between both companies that were provided from non-slaveholding households.

Company I marched from Franklin to Clinton, Tennessee, joining the other 8 companies of Coleman's Battalion. As of 14th April 1862, Crawford's Company had not yet joined the rest of the Battalion. The Battalion was having a major issue with large numbers of men succumbing to the sickness in the camp. Bell's Company of 95 had 18 men ready for duty around that time the sickness was so bad. From 7th-14th April 1862, the men were subjected to constant cold rain, and for 2-3 weeks leading up to it, they saw rain about every other day. The entire area of operation had turned into a mess of rain and mud. In Knoxville, the that were not sick found themselves camping without in mud and water.

It was at this point that Captain Bell voiced his first disdain for Colonel Coleman. Bell blamed the poor conditions and treatment of the men on Coleman and was actively organizing a group to vote him out of his position as Colonel. Bell alleged that Coleman had a severe drinking problem, among other things. Bell also criticized the man which Coleman had appointed as Major after taking his Lt. Colonel promotion. Bell referred to Major Thomas W. Peirce, who Bell alleged; "is a fool and has no sense besides."

Over the next few weeks, the men continued to fight massive sickness. But during this time, it was clear that Coleman's Battalion would soon be formally designated as a regiment. The politics of the situation were nasty. Within the companies, officers were "Politicking" to maintain their positions as Captain and Lieutenants, but there was a major divide among the regiment. On one side were Colonel Coleman and his faithful, and on the other side was Captain Bell and his followers, who wanted very severely to oust Colonel Coleman. Within Bell's Company, Thomas Roane was elected to 2nd Lieutenant instead of Joshua C. Bird.

At the Regimental level, Captain Bell wanted the command to go to the infamous William Holland Thomas of Jackson County. Among the captains, Coleman had the support of Company G's Paschal C. Hughes, who was also from Macon County, Company D's Ambrose Gaines, who was from Buncombe like Coleman, and Coleman's right-hand man from Company C Hugh Harvey Davidson, the Sheriff of Cherokee County. On Bell's side were allegedly Company A, Bell's Company, Company E of Clay County, and Company F, which was one of the assembled companies. Apparently, the companies in favor of Coleman had plenty of their men present, which Bell felt Coleman had sent a lot of the Lieutenants away, so their votes could not be counted. There is no evidence to prove or disprove that theory.

Bell had it figured that the opposition had Coleman beat 15 to 12. On 19th May 1862, Crawford and Company I arrived from Macon County to become the 9th company of Coleman's Battalion. Bell quickly got to Crawford and his officers to explain the importance of the vote and denigrate Colonel Coleman's name. Crawford and his officers had literally just joined the battalion and had no opinion either, but apparently, they told Bell they would take his word for it and vote the way he told them to.

Coleman allegedly called for Crawford and his officers to also explain their side of the election. Bell alleged that

Coleman and Davidson instructed Crawford that if Crawford and his officers would vote for Coleman and Davidson, they would vote for Crawford as Major. Bell felt that Crawford sold out his friends for higher rank. Bell himself was a candidate for Major but, as a result of Crawford's "pact", instead put the son of General Alexander Reynolds in for Major. Whatever the circumstances leading up to the election went, when it was all said and done, Coleman won as Colonel, Hugh Harvey Davidson won as Lieutenant Colonel, and Frank A. Reynolds won as Major.

Chapter 4

Captain Bell berated Crawford vehemently, "I have never seen a man look so bad. His men and several others are cursing him and say they would not vote for him again for corporal. I am not sorry for him. Had he stuck to his friends, he could have been elected to any position that we would have agreed on, but no, he is for office, regardless of his friends or the wishes of the men and just coming in a stranger to a large portion of our regiment and take sides against his own county boys and succeeding in getting them against him. He ought to have known that it would ruin him at home as well as here. They have made a tool of him, and we all laughed at him a great deal for selling himself to treacherous men. He is done politically good with many of his own men, and all the sharpshooters are out and eternally against him henceforth and forever."

That is an angry man. The words are so disparaging, and the sad part is that they are one side without hearing Crawford defend himself. Here is Crawford's side, in my view, as best as I can give it. Bell was not at Chickamauga, and he followed the army in the rear during the Atlanta campaign, all the while expressing great interest in getting out of the army. Crawford, on the other hand, was at Chickamauga, got shot in the Atlanta campaign, led the regiment at Nashville, and in the very last battle for the 39th Captain, Crawford was alongside 9 of his men and 17 of

Bell's. Maybe Crawford did not vote the way Bell wanted him to, but other than Bell's finest hour at Murfreesboro, Crawford seemed to embody a stronger character of service as the war progressed. That is my defense of a disparaged man who has been dead for 132 years and is not here to defend his name.

On 19th May 1862, the 9 companies stationed at Clinton, Tennessee was officially designated as a regiment of troops and assumed the designation of the 39th Regiment of North Carolina Troops. They were mustered in as a regiment of infantry. When they were formed, the 39th North Carolina had not yet seen combat, but already 5 Macon County men had died of disease. From Clinton, the newly minted 39th North Carolina was ordered to return to Knoxville, Tennessee and went into camp at the old fairgrounds.

On 1st July 1862, a young Jewish Cajun arrived after being a cadet at West Point for 2 years. His name was 2nd Lieutenant Isaac S. Hyams, and his time at West Point had been interrupted by the war. Hyams was given the daunting task of improving the drill of the 39th North Carolina and training the men in infantry tactics. Hyams, I am sure, was not very popular initially as he had to be the disciplinarian for a regiment of Stubborn Mountain men. Hyams, despite what they thought of him initially, I am sure the men gained respect for him as drillmaster.

If not, then I am certain they came around when he was recognized for his gallantry and distinguished service at Murfreesboro and Chickamauga. The men learned he didn't didn't just spit and polish, he was also a hell of a fighter.

There was little excitement in the summer of 1862. The men drilled and pulled guard duty in a constant, repetitive cycle. The men that grumbled through drill and guard duty were the lucky ones, though. The other men were horribly sick. In Macon's two companies, they had 20 men die of the disease in the hospitals around Knoxville. The 20 of Macon's sons died without ever seeing battle, and sadly, that summer's sickness was equal to the 20 men that Company B and I lost in combat. In about one month, 24 percent of their total deaths occurred. Among them was the brother of my grandfather Pvt. Joseph Beasley. On 14th July 1862, Pvt. William J. Beasley left an empty home in Cowee with his wife Rhoda and 5 children. William's body never made it home to Macon County. He is to this day buried in Bethel Confederate Cemetery in Knoxville, Tennessee.

My grandfather was in Crawford's Company, and William was in Bell's Company along with my grandfather's other brother Charles. In July of 1862, likely due to William's death, Charles was moved to Company I. On 8th February 1863, Charles was promoted to sergeant and served alongside his little brother for the remainder of the war. Also, in Company I was my other grandfather Pvt. Andrew

Jackson Stiles served in the company until he and his little brother William H. Stiles were surrendered at Citronelle, Alabama. My grandfather made it through the war without ever being wounded, but his little brother was injured in the shoulder and right arm in Atlanta. Joseph and Andrew were the first men that I learned of. They connected me to that misunderstood time period, and their story is why I wrote this book. As the Beasley brothers buried their brother in Knoxville, the 39th prepared to go on the offensive for the first time in the Invasion of Kentucky.

Act II

The Invasion of Kentucky

1 August 1862-30 December 1862

Chapter 5

In August 1862, the men of the 39th were assigned to General Alexander W. Reynolds' Brigade, of General Carter L. Stevenson's Division, of the Department of East Tennessee. Reynolds was, of course, the father of the Major of the 39th and a West Pointer Class of 1833. Reynolds was a Mexican war veteran, but several years after the war, he was dismissed from the army due to a large sum of money that went missing from his command. Reynolds fought and had his commission, along with his commission reinstated, but when the south seceded, Reynolds went AWOL from his assignment in Texas to fight with his home state of Virginia. He initially took command with the 50th Virginia before he was given command of a brigade.

General Carter L. Stevenson was also a Virginian and a West Pointer, but he was class of 1838. Stevenson was a veteran of the 2nd Seminole War and was on the Texas Frontier when the Mexican War Broke out. Stevenson made a name for himself during the Battles of Palo Alto and Resaca De La Palma. Stevenson also saw combat with the Apache while exploring the route for the Pacific Railroad. If that wasn't enough, Stevenson saw combat again in the Third Seminole War only to be moved out west, where he fought in the Utah War. When the south seceded, Stevenson also abandoned his post out west and headed home to Virginia.

By the time the Civil War began, Stevenson was a veteran of at least five separate conflicts. Stevenson was at first a Lieutenant Colonel, then received a commission as Colonel of the 53rd Virginia. As of August 1862, Stevenson was now in Command of General Smith's largest division, and that division was preparing for a large-scale invasion of the north. While the army of Northern Virginia was preparing to invade Maryland, the western Confederates were preparing to invade Kentucky. General Smith and General Bragg first met in Chattanooga, and General Smith turned his attention to his first objective: the Cumberland Gap.

As Smith moved toward the gap, he found that the Federal presence at Cumberland gap was too large and in too strong of a position. Instead of attacking the gap, he simply turned the other direction and headed toward Lexington, Kentucky. He left his largest division - that of Stevenson to guard the railways and lines of communication headed toward Knoxville and Chattanooga, and to contain the enemy within the gap, the rest of his command moved Northward on 24th August 1862.

On 30th August 1862, General Smith's 6500 Confederates were met by a Kentucky native named General William "Bull" Nelson and his 6850 Federals. Smith's army demolished Nelson's men. The Union Army suffered over 5300 casualties while only inflicting around 450 casualties on Smith's Confederates. General Nelson was wounded but able to flee to Louisville. Most of his army didn't make it as General Smith had over 4500 prisoners that he kept with him as he marched north. The battle was bad enough in losses, but the true cost was that Lexington and Frankfort were wide open.

On 1st September 1862, General Smith's army marched into Lexington unopposed to a warm reception of Lexingtonians lining the streets and cheering the army in. The people of Lexington were happy to be under Confederate control. As the union abandoned the city, they burned all of Lexington's government stores. I'm certain the people of Lexington were upset about such a thing, but there was also strong Confederate sentiment among the citizens of Lexington. Lexington stopped flying the American flag when Lincoln was elected and established Pro-Confederate Home Guards. Regardless of their reasoning, Lexington gave Smith and his 11000 strong Confederate Army a warm reception. General Smith messaged the Confederate Government that the heart of Kentucky had proven they were "with the south."

Kirby set up his headquarters at the old Phoenix Hotel at the corner of Limestone Main Street. He had to get to work paroling the 4500 some odd prisoners he had hauled from Richmond. Lexington was firmly under Confederate Control. Smith's men even put a Confederate flag up over the Fayette County Courthouse. There is always a staunch argument over when the Confederate high tide was. There are always arguments about whether it was Chickamauga or Gettysburg. I argue that it might have been in September of 1862 when the western army occupied Lexington, Lee was invading Maryland, and Confederates in Mississippi were marching to take back Corinth. This was the farthest the entire army was into enemy territory at one time. That's for certain; no other period comes close. In September of 1862, things were not looking good if you were for the union.

Trailing behind Smith was Bragg. Bragg took another route into Kentucky, which led him to Munfordville, Kentucky. At Munfordville, between 14th-17th September 1862, Bragg surrounded and completely choked off the Federal Garrison at Munfordville. Bragg demanded their surrender. Colonel John T. Wilder, in one of the craziest stories I'm aware of, asked if he could see the Confederate Line he was surrendering to. In an unprecedented, strange ride-along, Colonel Wilder and Confederate General Simon Buckner surveyed the Confederate force. Colonel Wilder and his odd ride found that around 25000 Confederates surrounded his 4000 Federals. On top of the Richmond Route and the capture of Lexington, Bragg had now captured another 4000 federals. The men of the 39th would find out almost exactly one year later that Bragg would have done them a favor if he had attacked Colonel Wilder that day. It isn't time for that story yet, though.

Meanwhile, the men of the 39th were still in Stevenson's Division and were far away from Munfordville, far away from Richmond, and couldn't see what Lexington looked like when Kirby's army marched in. They were instead pushed out on the line at Baptist Gap, Tennessee. While stationed there, the men were transferred from Reynolds' Brigade to the Brigade of General James Edward Rains.

Chapter 6

General Rains was a Tennessean and Yale Educated Attorney. Rains wasn't a West Point man like so many others, but the higher Confederate Command was noticing his actions in the gap. Being a private in April 1861 and now commanding a Confederate brigade should attest to the type of waves he was making in the army of the west.

The men of the 39th occupied the Confederate left near Baptist Gap, Tennessee, along with the 29th North Carolina, an unnamed Alabama Regiment, and elements of Thomas' Legion. The entire group was marched off to a gap south of Baptist Gap except for the Native American company of Thomas' Legion. They were left at Baptist Gap to protect the pass. The other three regiments were gone for 2-3 days to meet an expected Federal advance through that unnamed pass which never happened. As the men were returning and in the proximity of Baptist Gap, they could hear the Native American company firing heavily. The column quickly ran toward the gap, and once they got to the base, the column deployed a Skirmish Line forward. Lt. Davidson of Company C oversaw or at least was part of the front Skirmish Line as they moved forward to the gunfire. One of the Lieutenants of Thomas' Native American Company was also a chief of their tribe. As the men of the 39th moved forward, they found a squad of Thomas' Native Americans bearing off their chief that had been wounded severely. The lieutenant was named Lt. John Astoogatogeh. The lieutenant was the grandson of Chief Junaluska, who saved former President Andrew Jackson at the Battle of Horseshoe Bend. The grandson of Chief Junaluska died from his wounds later that evening.

The Native American company had been ambushed by a union forward reconnaissance group. The Native Americans, after having lost their chief, charged forward at the men and engaged them in vicious hand-to-hand combat. Conflicting reports attest that the Native Americans scalped some of their ambushers left behind wounded and dead. Lt. Davidson recalls that the Federals broke contact when they observed the other three regiments flooding the gap.

The day after what Lt. Davidson referred to as the regiment's "baptism of fire" revolved around a 100-man detail to clear timber off the road leading to the gap. Lt. Davidson led the Lumberjack company while Captain Dyce and Company A occupied one side of the gap while Captain Bell's Macon County men occupied the other. To the front of the detail was Davidson's Company and some of Thomas' Native Americans deployed further to the Union Line as scouts.

Thomas' Scouts captured at least three prisoners and brought them back to Lt. Davidson. The scouts wore traditional feather plumage and, at least in the eyes of their prisoners, were a frightening spectacle. Lt. Davidson ordered the scouts to take the men back to Rains' headquarters, but the frightened Union prisoners begged for a promise that they wouldn't be scalped. Davidson assured the men that they wouldn't be scalped. The men held the pass for several more days when a courier reported that General George W. Morgan's force had evacuated the Cumberland Gap. The men of the 39th took part in chasing the enemy after they abandoned the Cumberland Gap but never caught them.

The men of the 39th and the rest of Stevenson's Division were ordered to head north to join Smith in Kentucky. The army had been routed at Richmond, Smith occupied Lexington, Bragg had captured 4000 at Munfordville, and the Cumberland Gap was evacuated. The army of the west was on top of the world and still moving. The men of the 39th moved into Kentucky and were part of a much larger effort to secure sections of the new Confederate territory.

The men marched by way of Lancaster, then to Barboursville, Richmond, and then made their first major stop at Danville, Kentucky, where the men were put on guard duty. I have no official record of where the Macon men were detailed, but Lt. Davidson, two other officers, and 80 men were detailed to guard a large distillery owned by a prominent Union man. The confederate army didn't wish to harm union loyalists, as illustrated by their assignment; they were intended to protect his property at all costs. The man appeared quite delighted by the conduct of those men as, on one day, he provided the men with a huge feast.

The man and his three daughters sat 40 men at a time while the other 40 were on guard. They loaded down the hungry Confederates with turkey, chicken, and roasted pig. I can't imagine what a treat that must have been for men who were generally used for army rations and general deprivation. The men were formed up, and their march north continued. When the men formed up to leave, the Union men gave a thank you speech and filled all their canteens with four-year-old Rye Whiskey. As the men marched northward, they gave three cheers to the man and his family for their tremendous hospitality.

The men marched on through the darkness en route to Salvisa, Kentucky. Lt. Davidson cautioned the men to enjoy their canteen but to be careful with how much they drank. The interludes of sweating and hard marching go briefly better by quick shots of rye on the march. As the men marched on and some of the men would get broke down and fatigued, a quick shot of whiskey had them back in the ranks with a "bright step." At Salvisa, Lt. Davidson referenced that there had been a prior skirmish but that Salvisa was now in Confederate possession. Unfortunately, the rest of the 39th had already moved out, and Lt. Davidson could not find what direction they had gone as several Confederate commands had gone in several different directions but were all headed north. Lt. Davidson felt that a pike on the right-hand side was the safest and thus moved his detachment in that direction.

Chapter 7

About a mile up the road, Lt. Davidson and his detachment found themselves being stampeded by a squad of the 2nd Kentucky Cavalry (Confederate) under Major George Washington Morgan. Major Morgan and Lt. Davidson knew each other, and when Major Morgan saw Davidson, Morgan hurriedly instructed Davidson to get his men into a nearby thicket and hide until dark. Morgan instructed Davidson to slip out under cover of darkness and move up the Harrodsburg Pike. While hiding in the thicket, the Yankee Cavalry came storming by. The men hid well enough that the troopers didn't see them, and Davidson had no intention of bringing on an engagement. Major Morgan was wounded in a fight not long after at Ashland, Kentucky. Major Morgan died of wounds about 11 days later and is buried in Lexington, Kentucky.

As darkness fell, the men creeped out of the thicket and headed up the Harrodsburg Pike. The men marched through the night until about midnight, when they bedded down for a quick nap and ate breakfast around daylight. During the march, a lady brought corn cake and buttermilk to the men. Davidson ate so much of it that he made himself sick. The men arrived at Harrodsburg that night, where they found Davidson, a good manager in one of Kentucky's famous horse barns. Davidson had to sleep off the past several days' march and all the corn cake.

The majority of the Confederate army was encamped at Frankfort, which was about 34 miles north of Lt. Davidson's men at Harrisonburg. On 8th October 1862, the army of the Ohio engaged Bragg's army of Mississippi at Perryville, Kentucky. Perryville was a very small Kentucky hamlet, but it had several roads that connected to towns in several different directions, which was strategically enticing but at the root of it all was a very simple precious resource: drinking water. The area was in a devastating drought, and both armies wanted access to a large source of clean water. Perryville provided that.

Perryville was the biggest battle ever fought in Kentucky, and the union suffered over 4200 casualties, and the Confederates suffered over 2900. Around 1/5 of all men engaged were casualties. Perryville was mostly a stalemate, with both sides having claimed victory. Bragg had won a tactical victory in that he had met the union on the field and driven them back over a mile. He owned the field on the evening of 8th October 1862. Bragg didn't continue his push as he was concerned about the presence of two nearby Federal Corps. At around 21:00 on 8th October 1862, Bragg met with his subordinates and gave the order to withdraw after midnight back to Harrodsburg. Bragg developed a reputation for gaining early victories but not finishing them. This legacy haunts his legacy to this day. After a great deal of success in his campaign, and arguably another victory, Bragg did what he ordered; he withdrew to Harrodsburg.

Theodore F. Davidson was a Private in Company C and served as a quartermaster sergeant and sergeant major for the 39th. In his recollections of the 39th, I think he echoed the sentiments of many of the men in the 39th. Sergeant Major Davidson, not to be confused with Lt. Davidson, felt that General Smith's army was confused at why Perryville was abandoned while 30,000 of them were ready to fight but were never called on to fight. Sergeant Major Davidson rationalized that there must have been some reason, but he didn't understand it. Davidson specifically references that the army started to lose some faith in Bragg and his ability to lead an army.

The circumstances being as they were, Bragg and Smith retired to Harrodsburg. The 39th, along with the Rains' Brigade, acted as the rearguard to Smith's army, where they, along with Confederate cavalry, were engaged a few times during the retreat. Waiting for them at Harrodsburg was Lt. Davidson and his detachment of whiskey guards. The 39th wasn't engaged at any of the major battles of the Kentucky campaign but received their "baptism of fire" in several small skirmishes. In the grand scheme of things, I don't know if it's fair to call them skirmishes, as the Civil War had skirmishes where hundreds died. The men of the 39th were shot at, and they returned fire on their trip to Kentucky. Lt.

Davidson was reunited with his command at Harrodsburg, and in quick order, the entire command quickly moved toward Camp Robinson.

The 29th and 39th North Carolina men gathered on some straw piles on Sunday 12th October 1862 to a service conducted by the Chaplain of the 29th North Carolina. The union didn't allow for much rest as they were still in pursuit. The men marched past Camp Dick Robinson sometime in the wee hours of Monday morning. In the darkness, the men could see tons of fires that were burning commissary stores. The food had to be abandoned so quickly that instead of anyone eating it, they were being burned. Massive supplies of pork were being burned to the ground. Many soldiers couldn't stand to see it. Many men fixed their bayonets and broke ranks to raid the burning food. Men would plunge their bayonets into a burning ham and hoist them up on their shoulders for the trip.

Men familiar with starving must have been so sickened to see such large amounts of food being wasted. Oftentimes war is less about what you can have and more about what you can keep your enemy from having. Given their relatively small involvement in Kentucky's fighting, the men of Company B and Company I didn't have any wounded or killed, and seven Captured. The two companies had around five men die from circumstances not related to combat during the time the campaign took place, but I can only confirm that Pvt. William Bingham and Pvt. Alexander Hall died while in Kentucky. It also appears that Sgt. Nathaniel Vanhook died while the 39th was near Cumberland gap and hadn't yet crossed the Kentucky border.

Chapter 8

At the close of the Kentucky Campaign, both Armies occupied almost identical locations as when they started. Lee's army out East had been bloodily halted at Antietam, and the Bragg and Smith's Confederates had abandoned Kentucky. What was once an incredibly wonderful time for the Confederacy was over as quickly as it started. Bragg partially blamed the campaign on Kentuckians themselves. Bragg took extra rifles with him into Kentucky to arm all the new recruits he was going to pick up. He intended for the Kentucky volunteers to swell his lines by as much as 25,000 to 50,000. Bragg rallied around 2000 Kentuckians to his cause, and in a letter home to his wife, Bragg attested that around half of 2000 had deserted.

Despite not getting volunteers, Bragg and Smith had expelled federal troops from Northern Alabama and Middle Tennessee. It took the federal army a year to reconquer that ground. Perhaps the best benefit to Bragg/Smith's Invasion were the spoils of war. The army had eaten well during the invasion and brought back enormous amounts of supplies and vast herds of cattle, mules, horses. Bragg loaded his wagon trains down with Bacon, flour, guns, clothing, and ammunition. He also hauled back 35 federal cannons. It's easy to make an argument for and against Bragg's success in Kentucky. If victory were measured by provisions alone, the

Confederate army was in a much better position than when they first embarked.

The men of the 39th settled at Lenoir's Station, Tennessee, and went back to work preparing for their next adventure. At this time, a few key moves took place. Sergeant Major Davidson was relieved from his position as Sergeant Major due to his being underage. When he enlisted, Theodore was 16, and by the time the campaign in Kentucky was over, he was only 17 and wasn't set to turn 18 for another five months. On top of that, Sergeant Major Davidson had already served six months in the Buncombe Rifleman of the 1st North Carolina infantry. The Buncombe Rifleman was the first company raised for Confederate service west of the Blue Ridge Mountains, and he served alongside a Macon County man in company I named Pvt. William Avery Conley. The first company of mountaineers raised for Confederate Service contained a Macon County man. Davidson was moved to the Staff of General Robert B. Vance. As for the rest of the 39th, they got back to the normal duties of guarding bridges and continuous drill with 2nd Lt. Hyams.

The men of the 39th also got detached from Rains' brigade. Rains was awarded the rank of brigadier general prior to the battle of Murfreesboro, but his rank wasn't confirmed when on 31st December 1862, Rains was shot through the heart while leading his brigade forward against a Union artillery position. His final words were said to have been, "Forward, my brave boys, forward!" Although the 39th was no longer with him, the men of the 29th North Carolina were following him in battle when Rains was killed. Rains' body was originally buried on the field. His father, wife, and three-year-old daughter inquired through Union General Williams Rosecrans, which aided in the movement of his body to his final resting place in Nashville. Even though the 39th didn't serve with Rains at Murfreesboro, they found themselves in the rocky, forested landscape that was the Murfreesboro Battlefield.

Act III

The Battles of Murfreesboro and Jackson

31 December 1862-17 September 1863

Chapter 9

Following Bragg's invasion of Kentucky, Bragg's army of Tennessee had settled at Murfreesboro, Tennessee, as of 20th November 1862. Confederate President Jefferson Davis visited Bragg in mid-December and directed that the men of Stevenson's 7500 man division be moved to reinforce Vicksburg. I'm not exactly sure how exactly it came to pass, but the men of the 39th didn't move with their Brigade to Vicksburg and were instead ordered to Murfreesboro instead as a detached regiment. They were a "Bastard Regiment."

Bragg was in command of two corps at Murfreesboro under the commands of General Leonidas Polk and General William J. Hardee. General Bragg was never a popular man, and he tended to rub people the wrong way, but General Polk seemed to be the leader of the prevalent movement to relieve Bragg of Command. Polk was also very close to President Davis and petitioned for his removal, but Davis didn't relieve Bragg or any of the Generals that called for his removal. The command climate of the west at the highest levels was toxic, and toxicity is detrimental to battlefield success. The fact that the western Confederates dealt with such squabbling while men like Lee and Stonewall were beacons of leadership in the east is a great testament to how hard they fought for the victories they earned.

The Union side had its own problems as well. Lincoln was an ax man and had little patience for failure to act. Just as he went through Generals in the East, so too did Lincoln not hesitate when replacing hesitant Commanders in the west. Lincoln, prior to Gettysburg, replaced General Buell with General Rosecrans. Rosecrans concentrated his forces at Nashville, Tennessee, under warnings from Washington Brass that he too would be replaced if he failed to act quickly. Rosecrans still took time to organize his army with a special emphasis on his cavalry. Union cavalry was regarded as weak in both theatres, but in the West, General Forrest's cavalry was running circles around them.

On 26th December 1862, Rosecrans Army departed Nashville and moved in the direction of Bragg's concentrated force at Murfreesboro. Bragg's command straddled Stones River with Hardee's Corps on the east bank and Polk's Corps on the west. When Rosecrans Army departed Nashville, the 39th hadn't made it to the Murfreesboro battlefield. Rosecrans arrived in Murfreesboro on the evening of 29 December 1862, and by the time dark fully settled in, about 2/3 of Rosecrans Army had taken up a position along the Nashville Turnpike.

On the morning of 30th December 1862, 41,000 Union soldiers were across the field from 35,000 Confederate soldiers. One element of Bragg's defense that was not present across the field was his cavalry. Although Forrest wasn't a part of the actions at Murfreesboro, the Confederate cavalry was greatly superior to the Federal cavalry. While

Bragg and Rosecrans were sizing each other up, Wheeler and 2,500 Confederate troopers and literally rode around the Union Army the day prior. Wheeler's men took around 1,000 Prisoners, and many of Rosecrans supply wagons. The Confederate superiority in cavalry operations is what had slowed Rosecrans down in the first place. Despite his preparations, his cavalry was still ill-prepared to stand up to Wheeler's cavalry.

The two armies, as of 30th December 1862, were in parallel lines which stretched in length over four miles. As Rosecrans and Bragg formulated their plans of attack, they both had the same plan. Bragg sought to hit the right of the Union Line; Rosecrans sought to hit the right of the Confederate Line. Rosecrans intended to hit Bragg immediately after breakfast, and Bragg intended to hit Rosecrans at dawn. With both plans so similar, the path to the quickest victory seemed as if it would hinge on who acted first. The four-mile lines were situated around 700 yards from each other. As darkness settled on Murfreesboro the night of 30th December 1862, men on both sides had plans to attack the enemy the following morning. As men tried to get some sleep in the freezing cold, the men knew that when they camped the following night, they wouldn't all be there.

Both armies had barely risen on the morning of 31st December 1862. The weather was freezing, and a heavy frost was lying on the ground. The Union Army was boiling coffee and preparing breakfast before their planned attack on the Confederate right. As they rubbed sleep out of their eyes and desperately tried to get warm, all hell broke loose.

Around 06:00, the Confederate Corps under General William Hardee fired the opening shots of the Battle of Murfreesboro. Completely taken by surprise, the initial elements fled in confusion. Men were gunned down as they fled. Over 10,000 Confederates amassed on the Confederate left attacked in one giant wave. The charging Confederates swept everything in front of them, capturing artillery before they had the chance to fire a single shot. One of the first two Union divisions that were engaged suffered over 50% casualties during the assault while the other held briefly before also fleeing.

The attack was catastrophic and forced Rosecrans to abandon his attack and move those forces to reinforce his own right. Rosecrans rode on horseback across the lines directing various units back into line. While Rosecrans rode, his uniform was covered in the red blood of his chief of staff. His chief of staff was decapitated by a cannonball while riding alongside him. Rosecrans maintained his cool and was integral in restoring order to his line. Order at that point didn't mean much as his original line had been driven back approximately three miles to the rear.

Amidst the initial confusion, Bragg launched two more Confederate divisions of Polk's Corps to strike as part of the second wave. General Sheridan aided in keeping the entire army from being destroyed as he had put his division fully into line at 04:00 that morning. They weren't making coffee and cooking breakfast; they held the right center of the line against the second wave. Despite this heroic stand, Sheridan's division bore the weight of a complacent army. All three of Sheridan's brigade commanders were killed, and 1/3 of his brigade were casualties in four hours of fighting. By 10:00 and within the span of four hours, the Confederate army had achieved most of its objectives and, in doing so, had captured 28 cannons and more than 3,000 Union Prisoners.

Chapter 10

As stated in the beginning, the rest of their brigade was ordered to Vicksburg, and the 39th was completely alone, as in they weren't attached to anyone. The men of the 39th had to fend for themselves. The regiment showed up as the battle was already underway. Arriving at the field, Company I was ordered to load ammunition wagons as the rest of the regiment moved forward to the battlefield. It is unclear whether this was ordered by Coleman or if some higher-ranking officer ordered it when Coleman reported his regiment to the field. Without company I, Company B and the rest of the regiment proceeded toward the fighting.

Upon reaching the field, the Confederates were largely in command of the field as they had caused Rosecrans Line to collapse onto itself, which had formed a V. Polk was attacking the apex of the V strongly and all over the field despite the success, the Confederates were suffering extremely heavy casualties everywhere they were attacking…especially at an area infamously known as "the round forest."

The men were attached to Donelson's Tennessee Brigade and moved forward as part of Donelson's Advance. Donelson's Tennessee Brigade was moved forward as the support element for General Chalmer's Brigade of Mississippians. As Chalmer's Line advanced forward, their line was broken by the ruins of the Cowan House, which was recently burned down. Past the Cowan House, Chalmers sought to reform his brigade under a murderous crossfire from Union infantry and Artillery coming from Hazen's Brigade in the round forest. Chalmer was wounded by an exploding shell amidst the chaos, which led his brigade to retreat through Donelson's oncoming advance.

This retreat, coupled with the ruins of the Cowan House, caused Donelson to endure the same issue that Chalmers men had. His brigade was split into. Part of the brigade pushed west into the Cedar Woods and directly into the men of Cruft's brigade while the other pushed toward Round Forest and the men of Hazen's Brigade. The men that went into the cedars pushed back General Cruft's brigade of Kentucky/Ohio/Indiana troops. The men that went toward the round forest were stopped under a murderous fire from Hazen's Kentucky/Ohio/Indiana/Illinois troops.

At this point, history doesn't tell us exactly which direction the men of the 39th went. They were complimented for "good service" by the Colonel of the 16th Tennessee, which attacked the Round Forest but also were allowed to imprint an inverted cannon on its battle flag for its part in the capture of enemy artillery, which apparently only happened on the other side. We do have a Macon County man that was there with a firsthand account, though. Captain Alfred W. Bell, the dentist/druggist from Company B without any combat experience whatsoever, was now leading a company of Maconians in their first “real” combat.

Based on Captain Bell’s account, it seems that the 39th split in the same direction that the 16th Tennessee did. Captain Bell stated that the regiment went into action at around 1030. As they moved forward, the men of the 39th were under very serious shelling. The men ran forward as quickly as they could to a stacked fence where the enemy fired a volley which wounded Pvt. Wilburn F. Roane and First. Lt. William Anderson of Company B. Roane was wounded in the left thigh, and Lt. Anderson was wounded in his shoulder and groin. This is also the point at which Colonel Coleman was wounded severely in his right leg. The wound struck Coleman just above his boot and passed straight through his leg. Luckily it missed the bone. Here Captain Bell specifically references that the regiment along with the 16th Tennessee commenced fighting against “three batteries, two Kentucky Legions, and two Indiana regiments with about 6-8000 men about 800 yards in front of them.”

There was a Cherokee soldier in Company C by the name of Pvt. James Fair. Fair had a bullet rip straight through his blanket roll, overcoat, and Bible. The Bible was where the bullet ended its trajectory. I’m sure Fair felt he was saved by divine intervention. I mean, why wouldn’t he? It was a bullet that could have ended his life lodged into his Bible. I guess the only unfair part is why so many other men didn’t have the same good fortune. From a historical standpoint, this near wounding sheds some light on what the men of the 39th might have looked like in the field. The men hadn't been in battle yet, and he had an overcoat. Apparently, there was some sort of Issue done to the 39th. I guess it's possible that he got it in Kentucky, but all we can really do is speculate. The other interesting note is that he was wearing a bedroll. I would assume many men in the regiment would have utilized the popular Confederate bedroll to carry their camp gear with them as opposed to the knapsack.

Command of the regiment fell to Lt. Col. Davidson, who shouldn't have even been on the field as his resignation had been unknowingly accepted. Davidson could have walked home; instead, he was leading a regiment emerged in stiff combat. Davidson didn't have to consider it too long as around 1300; he too was wounded. Lt. Col. Davidson was shot in his right elbow, and the wound ranged from the elbow to about halfway to his hand. The minie ball shattered his bone severely. Coleman was evacuated to Knoxville, but Davidson developed a fever at the field hospital and couldn't be moved. Davidson was captured by the Union as a result. The man that could have just walked away before Murfreesboro took a severe wound and spent the next five months in Union Captivity. As a cancellation prize, Davidson was awarded the badge of distinction for his actions at Murfreesboro.

With Coleman and Davidson both incapacitated, Captain Bell of Macon County received a quick battlefield promotion and found himself in command of not just his own company but the entire regiment. Bell states that a relief column came through around 1400, which seems to further indicate the men took part in the attacks on the round forest. As Bell was in command of the regiment, it's likely the men were hidden among the dead cornstalks. The men likely laid in the prone as minie balls whizzed by, and shells exploded overhead. Whichever way they went, they were part of a brigade that suffered around 51% casualties during their assault. The men of the 39th were in their first full-scale battle, and it was a hell of a way to start. In some of Bell's earlier letters to his wife, he referred to his regiment as the "Bloodless 39th." This is to highlight how they hadn't got the chance to prove themselves in battle. In his letter to his wife after Murfreesboro, Bell explained, "So I will quit the battle Subject by saying I had rather not be in any bigger battles."

Chapter 11

Sometime that afternoon, we found another excerpt for the men of the 39th in the official report of General James Patton Anderson. Anderson was leading a brigade of one Alabama regiment and four Mississippi regiments. Anderson wrote that 2nd Lt. Isaac S. Hyams, the Drill Officer for the 39th, reported to him on the field as the regimental Adjutant. Hyams informed him that the 39th was currently under the command of Captain Bell as all their field officers were wounded and that they were further detached from the command they had been with earlier in the day. The Bastard Regiment was taken in by General Anderson and put into line on the right side of the 27th Mississippi.

General Anderson's brigade did take part in the capture of Federal artillery that afternoon, which might be when the 39th was awarded its inverted cannon. The losses of both Donelson's brigade and Anderson's brigade were heavy, but there is no definitive proof of exactly when the 39th stopped being in Donelson's brigade and started being in Anderson's brigade.

All we know is that Captain Bell had the company fallen back that evening, and they spent the night in ditches and behind breastworks. The total actions of the regiment on 31 December 1862 aren't known, but that evening ended in the "ditches." At these ditches is where Captain Crawford and Company I rejoined the regiment. Captain Crawford and the company apparently didn't keep loading ammunition wagons for very long and were ordered to meet up with the rest of the regiment. Captain Crawford took the Bastard Regiment idea even further by becoming a Bastard Company that couldn't even find its own regiment. Crawford's company was exposed to heavy shelling during the day, which led to the mortal wounding of First Sergeant John E. Moore in his arm and chest. Bell talked about Moore's wound in his letter, simply saying, "poor fellow, a piece of shell struck his arm and broke it." First Sergeant Moore died that evening from his wound. Moore was awarded the Badge of Distinction for his actions at Murfreesboro.

The rest of the night was spent freezing in a cedar thicket, concealed behind breastworks and huddled in the ditches. The grapeshot and shells exploded all through the night around them and above them. When the men weren't on guard, they tried the best they could to get some semblance of sleep amongst all the horrifying sounds around them. The 39th had done a pretty good job of carrying their wounded off the field as quickly as they were wounded, but they had left behind the First Lt. John W. Rhea of Cherokee County and First Sergeant John Whitaker of Buncombe County on the field dead. The two men were the only men of the 39th killed in action, but after First Sergeant Moore died from his wounds, that meant the 39th had lost one Lieutenant and two

First Sergeants. Bell sent a burial party back where the regiment was engaged to bury the two men.

If there was any positive to the exploding shells they were subjected to, it was that the loud sound temporarily drowned out the screams of agony from the wounded. Men on both sides were detached in squads to round up the wounded, but that sort of work was dangerous even if the other side wasn't trying to kill you. It's not as if the entire army could just stop and go round up all their wounded. The parties which were dispatched weren't sufficient to make an honest attempt at curtailing the number of neglected wounded. Men screamed for mothers, God, and water and just generally cried out, seeking help from anyone. As they lay there begging for help or dragging themselves off the field, they had to navigate a sea of dead bodies. With upward of 25,000 casualties, no amount of descriptive writing or Hollywood Budget could ever illustrate that level of carnage.

Captain Bell described the scene in his letter home. Bell stated, "I saw hundreds of dead yanks someplace that I could walk on them in some places from 50 to 100 would be lying close together." He also stated that "I saw but few of our dead." The Battle of Murfreesboro/Stone's River continued for the next two days with more inconclusive fighting. After being presented with the facts of the battle, the Southerners won the first day's fight, no one won on the second day, and the Federals won the third day as Bragg's attack was pushed back with heavy casualties. Neither side scored a decisive victory at Murfreesboro, but Bragg abandoned the field on 3rd January, 1863, and, in abandoning the field, yielded the field to Union control. Just as he had at Perryville, Bragg scored tremendous initial success…but then he stopped.

In the post-war years, regimental historians didn't understand why exactly command fell to Alfred Bell. No other regimental historian had much to say about it, and as far as I can tell, they weren't present. The men froze in the cedars, and as they marched in the retreat, the army was being slammed by cold, rain, and mud. The mud made the march that much harder on the men. Captain Bell, by his own admission, fell out of the march. Bell, at some point, was able to get ahold of Major Reynolds' horse which is the only way he was able to make the trip. Bell relayed to his wife, "I hope the Maj. Will come soon and take his command." This at least answers the question of why the Major didn't take command when Coleman and Davidson fell…he wasn't there to do it. Perhaps some of the captains weren't present, or perhaps in the heat of battle, Bell just naturally took the helm. Whatever the case, a Macon County man, took Charge at Murfreesboro.

The reported losses of the 39th at Murfreesboro were two Killed, 36 wounded, and six missing. Given that I don't have a report of how many men the regiment took into battle…I'm unable to yield a casualty percentage. Of the 36 wounded, as you already know, First Sgt. Moore died of his wounds and was the only known casualty in Company I. According to Captain Bell, Company B took himself, Lt. Anderson, and 50 men into battle. Bell also claims that his company was the biggest Company present. Bell reported that in his company, he had None Killed, 16 wounded, and four missing. This means that the Macon County men minus the men of the company I sustained 38.46% casualties. The Battle of Murfreesboro was the Sixth Bloodiest Engagement of the War, with nearly 25000 casualties. At Murfreesboro, 31.43% of all engaged were casualties; so, in the sixth bloodiest engagement of the war, the men of Macon County experienced 22% higher casualties than average. There were more casualties at Gettysburg but to put perspective on how intense the fighting was for the men of the 39th, the casualty percentage at Gettysburg was 30.86%.

Writing to his wife, Bell talked specifically about four more of his wounded besides Wilburn Roane and Lt. Anderson. He refers to Pvt. Washington G. Thomas being hit by a piece of shell in his left shoulder, Pvt. Jesse T. Gregory was wounded in the right arm by a minie ball which had to be amputated, Pvt. William A. Thompson was wounded in the head and Pvt. John Guy had his left leg broken. The men of Macon County could finally say they had been in full-scale combat. The 39th had suffered its first three combat deaths, and of course, First Sergeant Moore, one of Macon's sons, was among the dead. John left behind a wife and two young daughters in Macon County.

Chapter 12

Following the Battle of Murfreesboro, the regiment settled at Shelbyville, Tennessee. They marched there as part of General Anderson's brigade but while there were transferred to Robert Vance's brigade of John McCown's Division. The men of the 39th found themselves brigaded with the 29th North Carolina under the leadership of Robert B. Vance of Buncombe County, North Carolina. This command, as great as it sounded, never actually happened, though. The men were instead put into the brigade of General William B. Bate of General Alexander P. Stewart. While at Shelbyville, the men got a good break. Also, while at Shelbyville, the 39th received reinforcements by way of Company A of the 16th North Carolina, which was a Company that had been raised out of Jackson County.

The men of the 39th found themselves back to camp life, drill, and the never-ending cycle of guard duty. Lieutenant Hyams no doubt went back to the less than desirable work of drilling stubborn mountaineers. General Stewart commanding the division issued orders for thorough training of the Company Officers, and with the help of some of the many former West Pointers in the army, the officers were trained in Hardee's Light Infantry Tactics. Of course, this book was written by none other than one of the Corps Commanders at Murfreesboro by the name of William J. Hardee.

Lt. Davidson of Company C was one of these Officers and apparently made a pretty good impression on his instructor as, within a few days, General Stewart seemed to take a special interest in Lt. Davidson. On the day prior, Stewart and his staff walked with and observed the movements of the 39th on the drill field. At the conclusion of their drill, Stewart thanked the men for their proficiency and gave them a classic "pep talk" to commend them for their improvements and commitment.

The following day, Colonel Coleman formed up his regiment and gave the order; "Order Arms, Parade Rest." Initially, the men felt relieved that they were given the order to rest instead of getting trotted around the old drill field. Soldiers don't like to drill today, and they didn't like to drill then. There was much relief throughout the ranks. As the men stood there, General Stewart and staff walked straight in front of the ranks of the 39th. General Stewart was saluted by the Staff Officers, and several of the Staff Officers of the 39th entered a "huddle" with him and his staff. There isn't a record of whom was in the huddle, but Coleman, Lt. Col. Reynolds, and the Adjutant First Lt. James D. Harden were there because when the conference was over, Lt. Harden stepped in front of the regiment and gave the following order: "Lieutenant J.M. Davidson, Company C, will take charge of and drill the regiment."

Lt. Davidson was not thrilled in any way about drilling the entire regiment. Davidson darted to Colonel Coleman and Lt. Colonel Reynolds, inquiring for advice. They simply told him to walk the regiment through any iteration of commands that he could. Davidson nervously gathered his thoughts and took his place at the front of the regiment. Davidson decided on a movement he found particularly "beautiful" and proceeded to order the men straight into the action without first giving them the preparatory command. For those that have never been on the Drill Field, simply understand that the Unit is so disciplined in its movements that a military unit can't move without a clear, exact sequence of commands. As Davidson failed to execute this command, the Unit stood still. Davidson was puzzled as to why the men still stood without moving. As the force grinned toward him, their faces were silent, but it was as if he could hear their smiles taunting him.

Quickly realizing his mistake, he tried again. Davidson yelled the correct commands, and the regiment wheeled about the drill field extremely well. Davidson built up some confidence then decided that he would really showcase his skills. Davidson went to deploy the column into the line of battle. This command is done quickly at a fast trot to quickly deploy the men and quickly prepare a Unit for battle. Perhaps in his excitement, Davidson stepped backward and got his feet caught up in a little bush. Davidson plunged to the ground hard, and his sword went flying out of his hand into the air and lodged in the ground.

As Davidson lay on the ground, he heard General Stewart, "Rise, Captain, and try it again." Davidson was never recorded as being a Captain, also at that time, Captain Mount was there, so I don't know if referring to Davidson as Captain had any meaning to it or if it was just a mistake either by Stewart or by Davidson's storytelling. Davidson collected himself and went to fetch his sword from the dirt. Davidson got the regiment back into line and then begged General Stewart to relieve him of command. General Stewart said that Davidson could be relieved and that other than the fall, he did a fine job.

General Stewart wasn't done, though. General Stewart next called out William Allen. William Allen was the Captain of Buncombe County's Company D. Company D was known as the Highland Greys, and Davidson recalled that Captain Allen was in possession of a very feminine tone in his voice. I picture one of those classic soft southern voices that used to be a lot more prevalent. Captain Allen attempted the same exact maneuver which Davidson had led the men in. However, Allen gave the wrong command, and it caused the men to rapidly change direction toward a dense stand of cedars. Allen, as the point, was in panic and froze up, not knowing what to say or do to stop his ill-executed command.

A man in the ranks was said to shout, “Down on your marrow bones and charge the cedar thicket!” Allen, in his feminine voice, shouted to the Colonel about what was wrong with the men. Colonel Coleman yelled back to Allen that the men were simply obeying what he told them to do. Allen yelled back at Coleman, “Colonel, for God’s sake, stop them and get them out of that thicket!” Colonel Coleman took over and executed commands that brought the men back to the center of the drill field. Allen, despite his initial crisis, led the drill successfully for a while thereafter. Captain Allen made it through the war but was murdered at his home by pillagers after the war.

Brought again to the center of the drill field, General Stewart again addressed the men, thanking them this time for the amusement. Stewart had led a brigade at Shiloh in the famous hornet’s nest. When Stewart told the men that soldiers deserved to have some fun, he meant it. Stewart had seen fighting as hard as anybody had up to that point in the war. That was the first time Davidson had to lead drill, and it was also the only time.

Chapter 13

The men of the 39th had a little bit of downtime in the winter of 1863 after their first battle, but it was ending. General Leonidas Polk was preparing his army for a movement, but prior to their departure, Polk took the opportunity to do a parade review of his entire corps. Polk was a native North Carolinian, and at his review stand, he chose the flag of the 39th North Carolina to be on full display. The flag had been presented to the 39th by some ladies from Asheville, North Carolina.

The flag was very original and not anything like any of the other regimental flags, and perhaps due to its nod to the Scottish ancestry of the regiment, Polk, also being Scottish, really took a liking to it specifically. Also on the flag was a nod to the Cherokee Heritage inside of the regiment. The flag was beautifully made. As the men of the 39th marched across the parade field, the flag was being carried by Sergeant William Breeden of Company C.

As the men marched, a man lost to history shouted, "Hurrah for the tar heels." This note is very important as the name tar heel is the source of a major debate. Where did it come from? The stories are many, but most people think the name started during the Civil war. Many of North Carolina's generals and officers had gone to the University of North Carolina long before the name "Tar Heel" was applied to it. The University of North Carolina adopted the name in 1893, which of course, is roughly 28 years after the Civil War. The most popular form of the story is associated with General Robert E. Lee. There was allegedly an exchange where a North Carolina soldier jeered a soldier from another state that if they'd put some stick tar on their heels, they could have held the ground and that North Carolina wouldn't have to retake the ground. Upon hearing this, Lee allegedly said, "God Bless the Tar Heels."

The term Tar Heel is meant to reference how well North Carolina soldiers "stick in a fight." The idea that the name came about in the civil war is at least supported in the 39th as when Lt. Davidson was telling the story; he mentions that the 39th didn't know about their "new name." Given that Sergeant Breeden wasn't yet aware of the term "Tar Heel," he took great offense to the man that yelled out the word.

Sergeant Breeden angrily rammed the staff of the flag into the ground and stepped away from the ranks of the 39th, and put his fists up like he wanted to fight. Breeden shouted that if anybody wanted to insult North Carolina that they needed to step out of ranks two at a time, and he would beat the entire regiment by himself. There was a tense few seconds that yielded to an eruption of laughter between both regiments. Breeden, at that point, realized the joke and snatched up his banner, getting back into line. As the corps marched, they reportedly made a fine display. Most important to the men was the large number of Shelbyville ladies that were in attendance. Soldiers never change, and I'm certain that the army was full of puffed-out chests and gawking eyes.

On 12th May 1863, about five months after the Battle of Murfreesboro and eight days after Lt. Colonel Davidson arrived at City Point, Virginia for exchange after his wounding and subsequent imprisonment, the men of the 39th were ordered to Mississippi. The men marched along with their North Carolina brothers of the 29th North Carolina, and the regiments arrived at Jackson, Mississippi, on 18 May 1863. Federals had evacuated the state capitol just two days earlier. The stay in Jackson was short-lived as the regiments were immediately ordered 30 miles to Canton, where General Joseph E. Johnston was organizing an army to relieve Vicksburg. At Canton, the 39th was assigned to the brigade of a North Carolina native by the name of General Evander McNair and assigned to the Division of New Jersey Confederate General Samuel French.

General Johnston didn't arrive in Mississippi until 13th May 1863 but then spent about two months preparing to help Vicksburg. The town of Vicksburg waited in vain for a relief column that never came. On 3rd July 1863, white flags of surrender started going up at portions of the Confederate line, and Grant and General Pemberton met to go over the conditions of surrender. As Grant and Pemberton negotiated the surrender of Vicksburg, General Lee was fighting the 3rd Day of Gettysburg in Pennsylvania.

Around 1000 on four July 1863, General Pemberton surrendered Vicksburg along with over 27,000 men, 172 cannons, and approximately 60,000 muskets. On four July 1863, Vicksburg had fallen, and Lee had just been defeated at Gettysburg in his last invasion of the North. General Johnston's relief column was near Vicksburg at the time of surrender but was far too late. The men of the 39th were at the Big Black River, which was around 25 miles from Vicksburg. On hearing of the surrender, Johnston quickly marched his army back to occupy the fortifications of Jackson. It is unclear why Johnston, in nearly two months, never got his army to Vicksburg to help, but he didn't.

The weather in July of 1863 was miserably hot. Both Armies were marching as fast as they could through blistering heat and amongst a drought. The same drought conditions that caused so many problems at Murfreesboro were worse and hotter owing to the time of year and that region of Mississippi being so generally hot. All the red roads were nothing but dust, and wherever the armies went, they were stirring up large red clouds from all the shuffling feet. The heat was bad enough without also choking the armies in the dust.

As Johnston had moved to Jackson, the army had left dead carcasses of cattle, hogs, and sheep in bodies of water along Sherman's routes to spoil what little water Sherman could find. Johnston's Cavalry was also successful in ambushing Sherman's crossings of the Big Black River, which allowed Johnston more time to fortify Jackson. Johnston's armies took to the work of shovels and picked and dug in as deeply as they could at Jackson. Johnston utilized soldiers from his army, local slaves, and Jackson civilians to dig all day in the blistering of 8th July 1863. Johnston bolstered his defenses by reinforcing his line with cotton bales, and on 9th July 1863, Johnston sent the slaves and civilians away, and his soldiers occupied his improved fortifications.

Sherman's army arrived on the outskirts of Jackson, Mississippi, on 9th July 1863 and approached Johnston's position on 10th July 1863. Sherman was hoping that Johnston wasn't going to offer to fight at Jackson. As Sherman's lead elements entered Jackson, they immediately started being shelled. Sherman's question of whether Johnston intended to fight was answered. Sherman didn't commit his force and instead commenced siege operations and conducted recon of Johnston's position. Sherman found that the fortifications had been improved and extended since the last time he'd met Johnston at the first battle of Jackson, and now the position was too strong to assault. Sherman commenced a strategy of heaving shelling and began digging his own positions in front of Johnston's line.

In addition to this strategy, Sherman began probing different points of the Confederate Line to determine strength. General Sherman thrust one of his 13 Divisions on the Confederate against the Confederate picket line of the First Arkansas Mounted Rifles of McNair's brigade, which, of course, included the 39th. A picket line was no match for an entire division, and after firing on the Sherman's Division under Alvin Hovey, the division put part of the 16th Ohio Battery into line and forced the pickets back to the mainline.

On 12th July 1863, the Union made its most concerted effort at breaking the Confederate line. Colonel Pugh's Illinois brigade was ordered forward with Colonel Bryant's brigade in Reserve. As Colonel Pugh proceeded forward, he didn't feel good about the ground to their front and called his division commander to inspect. After conferring with Colonel Pugh, Pugh's men were still ordered forward. During the conversation, artillery was called up and began shelling the Confederates. The Confederate line soon answered, and a "lively duel" commenced. Colonel Pugh reluctantly moved forward through the cornfield to his front and passed through a stand of timber, at which point he ordered his brigade to halt. In front of Pugh's brigade was a constructed killing field complete with felled timber which had been used to construct barriers that were designed to slow down infantry units.

Meanwhile, Hovey's brigade had also moved forward and pushed the Confederate picket line in that area back to the fortifications. Hovey moved more artillery into line and began digging in. At this point, the same Division Commander that ordered Colonel Pugh forward...General Jacob Lauman ordered his men forward into the trap that had been set by Johnston's Confederates. As Pugh's brigade moved into the open, they came under a murderous attack from Confederate Artillery.

In addition to the horrifying artillery attack, the men of the 32nd Alabama Infantry and 19th Louisiana Infantry also opened on the men working their way slowly through the Confederate obstacles. The men, despite the heavy firing, continued forward to about 80 yards from the Confederate line. The charge didn't accomplish anything but more death. The Confederates on that part of the line suffered 50 casualties and inflicted 508 casualties on Pugh's brigade of about 880. That's a casualty rate of 57.72%.

The survivors fled in confusion, with General Lauman among them. General Ord was Lauman's first line superior and found Lauman in complete disarray and unable to take control of what was left of his command. Lauman was unable to execute orders given to him by Ord, and in such a vulnerable state, Ord immediately relieved Lauman of command and thus ended Lauman's Military career, which up until that point had gone quite well. There are a million fingers that can be pointed at Lauman in this situation, but without diagnosing that too much, the only positive thing is that his disastrous charge proved the strength of the line at Jackson and fully affirmed that no subsequent assaults would be made.

The bodies from Lauman's assault sat in front of the Confederate earthworks for the next two days in front of the Divisions of French and Breckinridge. The men of the 39th doubtless took part in the slaughter of Pugh's brigade as they were in that part of the line, and a unit from their brigade is named specifically in the report. In Lt. Davidson's recollections, he states that as the Union line moved forward that the Confederate batteries on the line were concealed by cotton bales and brush. As the Union men advanced forward with four lines in perfect order, as they approached the line, the Confederates threw back the cotton bales and brush and fired their six cannons all at once. Davidson stated that at the same time, Breckinridge's men emerged like ghosts and fired into the column as well, leaving 700 dead, and the survivors were sent fleeing to the rear. No other place on the field experienced casualties like that. The scene that Davidson observed was surely the exact scene I relayed above.

What was left behind were the bodies of the dead in the intense Mississippi heat. They sat there rotting for two days. The bodies bloated and exploded in the heat. The putrid smell was so bad that the Confederates could hardly stand to stay in the trenches. The smell became so overwhelming that Johnston had to request a two-hour truce in order to deal with the decaying corpses. Sherman agreed to the truce, and men from both sides entered the area between the opposing lines and went about the work of dealing with the bodies. Former U.S. Vice President General Breckenridge's Division bore the gruesome detail.

The men of the 39th didn't get hit by any other major assaults but instead occupied the skirmish line and trenches as Sherman outmaneuvered Johnston and completely cut him off. Lt. Davidson recalls that Sherman's shells streamed through the air at night like meteors. The Union shells made whizzing sounds as they flew on their way to blow up Jackson homes and businesses. Johnston, despite being cut off, was extremely good at moving an army and was able to slip away and evade capture, which he did on 16th July 1863.

On the morning of 17th July, 1863, Sherman and his Union Army occupied Jackson. Sherman allowed Johnston to go peacefully, citing that instead of taking his army through the blistering heat, dense dust, he would instead do what Sherman did best…destroy. In his own words, "I will perfect the work of destruction and await orders."

The men of the 39th, for their part in the Battle of Jackson, were allowed to imprint the word Jackson on their battle flag to signify their active involvement in the battle.

It's highly likely that while they were at Brandon, Mississippi that men from the regiment painted the word onto their flag, which already read Murfreesboro. The men stayed at Brandon until they, along with other Confederate Units in Mississippi, were ordered to reinforce Bragg. The men of the 39th moved by train to Ringgold, Georgia, where they arrived on 17 September 1863. Upon arrival, the men stayed in McNair's brigade but left the Division under New Jersey Native Samuel French and were put into the Division of Ohio Native General Bushrod Johnson. The 39th was again serving under a Confederate General that was born in the North. With their assignment to General Johnson's Division, thus ended their Mississippi Campaign of 1863, and now they were around 13 miles away from Chickamauga, Georgia.

Act IV

The Battle of Chickamauga

18 September 1863-20th September 1863

Chapter 14

The men left Ringgold, Georgia, in the wee hours of 18th September 1863 en route to Chickamauga along with their North Carolina brigade Commander and Ohio Division Commander. The men of the 39th marched along Lafayette Road to the intersection of Graysville and Reed's Bridge Road. Oftentimes Chickamauga is only credited with being a two-day battle, but on 18th September 1863, the 39th went into action early in the morning along with the rest of Johnson's Division.

The men of Johnson's Division were moved to cross Reed's Bridge and attack the left flank of Rosecrans army. Tasked with guarding Reed's Bridge were three regiments, one Battalion of Cavalry, and two guns under the command of Colonel Robert Minty. Minty was a Native Irishman and former ensign in the British army. Johnson deployed his brigades with McNair's containing the 39th on his left, Fulton's brigade in the center, and Gregg's brigade on the right. A brigade from Hood's Division occupied the rear, and with Johnson's Division distracting Minty, General Nathan Bedford Forrest was able to move to the left of McNair's brigade and flank the Union right.

Minty had a skirmish line of the 4th Michigan Cavalry pushed out in front of his line that was quickly forced back into his mainline as Johnson pushed his division forward. On Minty's right was the 7th Pennsylvania Cavalry, his center was the 4th U.S. Cavalry, and the remainder of the 4th Michigan Cavalry occupied his right. Minty's line was facing a huge surge of Confederates and begged for reinforcements from Colonel Wilder's brigade that was also engaged at Alexander's Bridge. Wilder sent 7 Companies of his 72nd Indiana Mounted Infantry, the 123rd Illinois Mounted Infantry, and an Unknown number of extra artillery pieces. Despite Wilder's reinforcements, this wasn't sufficient to stop the Confederate line from advancing. As Minty's men fell back, Johnson's men pushed to within about one ½ mile of Lee's and Gordon's Mill. The men slept on their arms that night close to the front of Wilder's brigade.

Wilder is a name that I hope you remember. Bragg let him survey his lines at Munfordville, Kentucky, and he ultimately surrendered to Bragg's force. Wilder's men, despite being surrendered at Munfordville, were back in action, and they were now armed with Spencer repeating rifles. Wilder had mounted his infantry on every horse and mule that his men could find so that Wilder could get his forces quickly to the battlefield, dismount to fight, and then gallop off again to the next place they were needed. Wilder's brigade had become "The Lightning brigade." Wilder's ingenuity was Wilder's answer to Confederate Cavalry Superiority. Rosecrans army was slow to move due to Rosecrans's massive respect for Confederate Cavalry. Rosecrans had put elicited feedback from his army to create solutions, and Wilder had been one of the few Officers that offered anything.

Wilder also wanted his men to have Spencer rifles to give them an edge in battle, but the army wouldn't pay for it. Wilder asked his men if they would be willing to purchase their own rifles. The men unanimously agreed, and Colonel Wilder outfitted his brigade in Spencer Rifles via a personal loan. The result was 20 shots per minute per man, which was over 6x faster than their competition. Essentially, he turned his brigade into two Divisions, and a lot of army Corps were only equipped with two Divisions. It was like Wilder turned his brigade into a Corps. His plan was innovative. Get infantry there over 3x faster and less fatigued by mounting them, and when they got there, they had 6x more firepower.

Wilder was born a New Yorker, and his Great Grandfather and Grandfather were veterans of the Revolutionary War. His Great Grandfather had to have one of his legs amputated. His father was a veteran of the War of 1812. Wilder himself wasn't a Veteran like so many of the other men that he was fighting with and against at Chickamauga. Wilder owned a Foundry in Indiana and was an inventor that owned several patents. On the surface, he doesn't seem like the guy that would develop such an innovative unit but there he was on the fields of Chickamauga and ready to become a major thorn in the sides of the 39th North Carolina.

General Hood arrived on the battlefield on 18th September 1863 and assumed command over the column, which included Johnson's Division and Hood's Division which had been part of the reinforcements sent from Longstreet's Corps of the army of Northern Virginia. As the men bedded down for the Night, Hood ordered them to construct breastworks. Hood always had 1/3 of the men on guard while 2/3 of them slept. All through the night, the sound of axes and the rustling sounds of the dense forest could be heard as the Union Army scrambled to build up their fortifications. The Armies were facing each other along about a six-mile front which in most places had the Lafayette Road in between them.

General Longstreet hadn't yet made it to Georgia on 18th September 1863 and wouldn't make it to the field until around midnight on 19th September 1863. With Hood taking the command that would have been Longstreet's were he there, General Evander Law commanding one of Hood's brigade took charge of Hood's Division, and Colonel James Sheffield of the 48th Alabama took command of Law's brigade. The Confederate Left of the line from left to right consisted of Thomas Hindman's Division, Bushrod Johnson's Division, Alexander Stewart's Division, and Evander Law's Division. As Law's Division was forming into the line of battle, they were surprised when General Hood rode up and greeted his men. Law's division was under the impression that Hood was still in a Virginia Hospital recovering from his wound at Gettysburg. Hood's army wasn't amputated, but it was now useless. That didn't keep Hood out of the saddle. At around 07:30, General Bragg struck from the Confederate Right and the day opened with some of the most desperate and confusing fighting of the entire war.

Chapter 15

The Battle of Chickamauga resumed at around 07:30 on the morning of 19th September 1863 as Bragg's Right made the first attack. The men of the 39th as part of Hood's Corps occupied the left. When the battle opened, the men of the 39th could only hear the fighting in the distance. Later in the morning, the battle opened on the Confederate left as the skirmish line was pushed back to Johnson's mainline. Johnson's line was ordered to move forward and attacked the Division of General Jefferson Davis. Davis probably resented the fact that his largest claim to fame was the fact that he bore the same name as Confederate President Jefferson Davis.

Davis was a Mexican War Veteran and served at the Fort Sumter Garrison when the first shots of the war were fired there. He was there when it all started. If he didn't like being known as the guy that was named after the Confederate President, he replaced it with a more infamous title. He was the guy that shot General "Bull" Nelson and killed him after he felt that Nelson had insulted him. He demanded an apology which he didn't get, and found his only recourse was to take a man's life. Davis was initially arrested but was released due to the Union needing experienced field Commanders. The man literally got away with murder. Literally!

Davis' Division at Chickamauga consisted of three brigades under New Yorker Colonel Phillip Post, General William Carlin of Illinois, and the Norwegian Born Colonel Hans Heg of Wisconsin. The division consisted of seven Illinois regiments, two Indiana regiments, and a regiment a piece from Ohio, Wisconsin, and Kansas. Heg came from the lone Wisconsin regiment, the 15th Wisconsin, which went by the nickname of "The Norwegian regiment" or "The Scandinavian regiment" as most of their regiment consisted of Norwegian Immigrants.

As Johnson's Division moved forward into Davis' Division, Gregg's Tennesseans were on the left, Fulton's Tennesseans were on the right, and McNair's brigade was in reserve to the rear. As Johnson's "Division pushed forward, they succeeded in defeating a portion of Davis' Division, but the brigade under Heg counterattacked and made a strong stand and caused Gregg's Tennesseans to scatter and stalled the Confederate advance. General McNair detached two of his regiments to the left to counterattack Heg's brigade. The 39th North Carolina and 25th Arkansas under Lt. Colonel Eli Hufstedler charged forward past Gregg's brigade and slammed into Heg's brigade.

As Coleman led the two regiments forward, the men were screaming at the top of their lungs. This move was enough to break Heg's brigade and drive them back through the Woods and then across the Lafayette Road, which sent them pouring into Glenn Field past the Viniard House, and into the cornfields East of the Widow Glenn House where Rosecrans had set up his headquarters. During this assault, Lt. Colonel Hufstedler of the 25th Arkansas was shot five times and lay dead on the field. As the regimental colors raged forward in the hands of Sergeant William Breeden, Breeden was wounded in the hands and according to First. Lieutenant Cathey of Company K, Breeden "was shot down." As the colors hurled toward the ground, Lt. Cathey grabbed the regimental flag without allowing it to hit the ground.

Lt. Cathey proceeded forward with the flag until Corporal Joseph Sutton, also of Company K, pried it from the hands of his Officer and carried the flag forward. The Assaulting men of Coleman's Detachment had charged so hard and so fast that they found themselves far in advance of the rest of the Confederate line. If you go to the battlefield today, you can see the monument in Viniard Field that marks the location where Coleman's penetrated to. It is far in advance of the rest of the line. It was here that the two little regiments were subjected to a murderous fire from their left flank. It was Wilder's brigade and their Spencer Repeating Rifles. Here in the middle of the field, standing alone, were at best 286 men. This is assuming that everyone that wasn't a casualty made it to this point. I'm sure some number of men ran away, but at absolute best, there were 286 men being poured into by a brigade worth of men with a Corps worth of firepower. Bragg would have saved many lives in the 39th North Carolina and 25th Arkansas if he had just attacked Wilder in Munfordville, Kentucky. The men of the two regiments fell back to the Woods East of the Lafayette Road.

In the assault, Pvt. Lorenzo Bradley of Company C was among the killed. Bradley had been captured in Kentucky but had returned after he was exchanged. Bradley gave a note to Lt. Davidson to give to his mother. Lt. Davidson oversaw Colonel Coleman's and Lt. Colonel Reynolds' horses during the battle, so when the 39th moved forward, Bradley gave his note to Davidson, knowing he had a much better chance of surviving. Bradley had a dream the night before in which he experienced the entire circumstances of his death. He had it set in his mind that he had seen the way he would die, and he had come to terms with it. Lt. Davidson walked the portion of the field that evening where the 39th had gone into battle. About ten paces from where Bradley gave Davidson the note was a grouping of about ten dead bodies. Among them was a man that had fallen face-first into a large rock. Davidson rolled the man over to find Pvt. Bradley. Davidson unbuttoned his coat and found that Bradley's chest had been shot three times. Because Bradley was hunched over on his face, they must have all hit him in near unison. It's interesting that we know the story of Pvt. Bradley, but he wasn't alone. The 39th had already suffered more casualties than they had at the Battle of Murfreesboro, and the fighting wasn't over yet. When the fighting was over on Saturday, Joseph Sutton took the regimental flag that he'd ripped from Lt. Cathey's hands and gave it to Colonel Coleman. He told Coleman he preferred to carry a rifle. James Wesley Shelton of Jackson County volunteered to carry the colors and carried it from that day forward.

During the night, the temperatures got below freezing. Water froze in canteens, blankets were in the rear, and fires couldn't be lit as to hide troop positions. The wounded were largely left unattended to fend for themselves. If it wasn't already miserable to lie helpless in a field surrounded by corpses and other wounded, the men also didn't have access to water. Cries of despair and pleas for help filled the air throughout the night. Out of comfort and to keep warm, men slept among the bodies of the dead, even using them as pillows. There were thousands of corpses on the field. Blood was everywhere, body parts strewn everywhere, brain matter seeping from open holes, guts blown through bodies and stuck to trees, and the horrors of which are sights that no human being should ever have to see. The men of the 39th, the other Confederates, and the Union men had to see an amount of carnage that was unimaginable. I'm certain that the men that endured that long, cold night never forgot about it, and many of them lived with nightmares for the rest of their lives.

Chapter 16

The fighting was over for day 2, though, and the men of the 39th along with the rest of Johnson's brigade were back in the wood line to load up on ammunition, eat, and rest. The men went into camp for the evening. Hood's men advanced again on the enemy after Johnson's Attack and fought deep into the evening. As Hood's men marched forward, one of Johnson's brigade commander, General John Gregg, had his lifeless body lay on the ground to the front of Hood's advance. Gregg had been shot in his neck and drug by the reins of his horse. Union scavengers were in the process of stealing his sword and his spurs. Hood's men succeeded in driving off the scavengers and saved both General Gregg and his horse.

The advance drew the attention of Heg's brigade, which began hotly engaging the front ranks of Hood's advance. Hood's men also charged through Viniard Field and were also eventually driven back by Wilder's Spencer's. One of Hood's brigades, the Georgians of Benning's brigade, advanced into Heg's brigade, and Heg was wounded by Benning's Georgians. Heg was shot through his bowels and evacuated to a Union Field Hospital. Colonel Heg was in disparaging pain. Various Officers visited his bedside, which was hard for them to take as Heg was in agonizing, visible pain. The day after Heg was wounded, he died in the field hospital. Heg's men fell back into Colonel Wilder's line after their Commander was wounded. Hood's corps put in both of his divisions at two separate intervals, and both were driven back due to not having enough support. Perhaps if both Divisions had gone into line at the same time, it might have been enough, but history didn't go that way. Both Divisions of Hood's Corps were back in the same wood line they had first emerged from.

The first day of Chickamauga had seen horrible casualties without Bragg having taken control of the Lafayette Road or having blocked the Union from Chattanooga. On the other hand, Rosecrans hadn't driven Bragg from his original ground and back across the Chickamauga River. If ever there were a stalemate, it was 19th September 1863. As the men bedded down the night in, Hood again put his corps in a pattern of 1/3 of the men on guard, with 2/3 of the men able to bed down and once again built-up fortifications along his line.

General Hood moved back to General Bragg's Headquarters to report out to Bragg the same way that he had reported to General Lee back in Virginia. At Bragg's headquarters, Hood found former U.S. Vice President Alexander Breckenridge sitting under a tree. Hood was discouraged by the lack of motivation and enthusiasm for victory among Bragg's men. Hood exclaimed to Breckenridge that they would crush the enemy the following day, which brought about some excitement in Breckenridge that Hood could tell wasn't common among Bragg and his Officers. The command climate at the top of the army of Tennessee didn't seem to have a winning culture. Hood received orders that Hood was to attack the following morning after he heard the attack commence on the Confederate right. Hood moved back to his line and began preparing his troops for another day of battle.

Bragg, unhappy with the outcomes of 19th September 1863, fell asleep in an ambulance at his Headquarters. Longstreet had spent the evening making his way to the Chickamauga battlefield, navigating by the sounds of the fighting. Longstreet was nearly captured by Federal pickets but was able to evade capture and arrived at Chickamauga around midnight. Longstreet finding Bragg asleep woke him up to discuss Bragg's plans for the following day. Bragg had his army organized in a right-wing, and a left-wing and command of the left-wing was given to General Longstreet. After talking for about an hour and Longstreet understanding the same very basic idea that Bragg's right-wing under General Leonidas Polk would attack at Dawn. Ideally, Polk's advance would drive the Federals left, and General Longstreet's Corps having stepped off right after Polk fired his first shots, the Confederate army would rout the Union Line and cut off Chattanooga.

On the following morning, Dawn came and left without Bragg's Right-Wing initiating an attack. There was confusion among Polk's Wing. When Polk woke at 0500 on the morning of 20th September 1863, he was surprised to find that General Daniel H. Hill was not yet preparing for an attack. Hill was, in essence, demoted and was now under General Polk. At 06:00, Hill was ordered to commence the attack; Hill responded with a bevy of reasons that prevented his attack. Part of his reasoning was that his troops needed to eat breakfast first.

The attack finally commenced at 09:30 in the morning, about four hours after Bragg had intended. While Polk's Corps hit the Union Left, the men of the 39th were attacked by an advance on their fortified position at approximately the same time. The line repulsed the advance, and the Union elements withdrew. At around 11:00 issued a general order for the entire line to attack. In the tree line was a portion of Longstreet's Corps that consisted of around 11,000 men. The column consisted of a roughly 700-yard front organized into five lines. In the front line was Fulton's brigade on the left and McNair's brigade on the right. The men of the 39th were the fifth regiment from the left, which made them the very left of McNair's brigade. On their right was the farthest right regiment of Fulton's brigade; the 44th Tennessee.

The men of the 39th were in the very front of the line, almost directly in front of the Brotherton Cabin. Behind Fulton and McNair was Gregg's brigade that was now under the command of Colonel Sugg of the 50th Tennessee due to

Gregg's severe wound the previous day. Immediately behind Gregg were Law's Alabamians. Behind Law was Robertson's brigade of Arkansas/Texan troops on the left and Benning's Georgians on the right. Comprising the final line were Humphrey's Mississippians on the left and Kershaw's South Carolinians on the right. The column began moving forward at approximately 1110 on the morning of 20th September 1863.

Chapter 17

On the other side of Lafayette Road, there was a major issue. Rosecrans was exhausted, and his exhaustion might have aided in a major miscalculation on his part. Rosecrans perceived that he had a hole in his line and commanded that General Wood's Division be used to fill it. General Wood was cognizant of the fact that the only hole that would be in the Union line would be if he were to move his line. General Wood protested it initially and was told to execute the order anyway and was assured that the hole would be filled. Wood received the order at around 1050, which was approximately 20 minutes before Hood's Detachment of Longstreet's wing began their movement. At the time Wood began shuffling his troops, the column emerged from the woods and were pointed almost perfectly at the newly formed hole in the Union line.

Fulton's brigade went directly into the Gap, and McNair's men slammed into Colonel John Connell's Ohio/Indiana brigade. Connell's brigade was unable to hold as McNair's men continued to push forward. The column pushed steadily forward, routing the Union Right and sending them fleeing in panic. The Union Right was in a state of emergency and was crumbling fast. Small pockets of Union men stood and attempted to resist, but the Confederate Column was overwhelming. The men of the 39th pushed the enemy past two lines of breastworks and sent them flooding into the Dyer Field. The Confederate line was moving toward Rosecrans Headquarters.

The men of McNair's brigade were still pushing forward, and after having driven the enemy about 3/4 of a mile, the men found themselves in the corner of Dyer Field and again far in advance of the mainline and under fire from two batteries of Union Artillery which were wreaking havoc on the main Confederate lines advancing across Dyer Field. Around this time, General McNair was wounded by a shell fragment, and command of the brigade temporarily fell to Colonel Robert Harper of the First Arkansas Mounted Rifles. Colonel Harper was mortally wounded, and command of the brigade fell to Colonel Coleman of the 39th North Carolina. Colonel Coleman led the brigade diagonally to the right and engaged the Artilleryman in a short but desperate hand-to-hand contest, which resulted in the capture of 10 Union artillery pieces. The confrontation was so sudden and desperate that the Union men had to resort to hurling grapeshot at the surging Confederates to try and stem the tide.

Coleman's men found themselves in a vulnerable spot again, especially on their left flank. With a Union line drawn up in their front and a larger body forming up to their rear, Coleman's brigade abandoned their position and returned to the wood line to procure more ammunition. In the wood line, after loading up more cartridges, the men formed again on the left side of Robertson's Texas/Arkansas brigade.

Charles Dana was a secretary of war that Lincoln had sent as a spy to check up on Rosecrans. He was napping at Rosecrans headquarters when he was awakened by the noise of the furious charge that was headed their way. When Dana woke up, he saw General Rosecrans crossing his chest. When Dana saw the devout Rosecrans behaving this way, he knew his surroundings were not good. Rosecrans made a futile attempt to rally his fleeing army, but ultimately Rosecrans, future President James Garfield, his Chief of Staff, two of his Corps Commanders, and Secretary of War Charles Dana joined their army in their rush to safety. A large portion of the army of the Cumberland was in a mad dash to put Chickamauga behind them, but one of Rosecrans' Corps Commanders wasn't on the run. Virginia Native General George Thomas was the only Corps Commander left on the field.

General Thomas' men were still holding strong in the Kelly Field, and rogue elements of the Union Army were assembling at a strong defensive position on Snodgrass hill. As the defense started to grow stronger, men began throwing up breastworks using downed timber and brush. As more men took up defensive positions, more men began arriving, and large Union units began arriving, and the Reserve Corps under General Granger moved forward without orders to assist in defense of Snodgrass Hill. The presence of men was a godsend, but equally important was a large amount of ammunition that they brought which were used to resupply the men atop Snodgrass hill. These were the activities of the remainder of the Union Army at the same time as the various attacks and the procurement of more ammunition by the 39th. The fighting was desperate all along the line, and the Union Army was desperately trying to pull together a defense.

As Rosecrans and his other Corps Commanders were abandoning the field, Rosecrans and his Chief of Staff James Garfield discussed the need to prepare the defenses of Chattanooga. It's not exactly clear what exactly was said between the two. The result of the conversation was that Rosecrans headed for Chattanooga, and Garfield rode back to the battlefield. Rosecrans probably had already lost his command, but his retreat to Chattanooga might have been the final nail in the coffin. Garfield's ride ended with his horse dying at General Thomas' feet. James Garfield's ride is probably the catalyst that secured his future as the 20th President of the United States. Garfield delivered orders to Thomas to retreat; Thomas told Garfield that he would have to stay behind in order to ensure the safety of the army. This was when Garfield told Rosecrans that Thomas was "standing like a rock." This is the moment that established General Thomas' nickname, "The Rock of Chickamauga."

Chapter 18

Thomas was preparing remnants of a scattered army for the defense of Snodgrass Hill. Snodgrass Hill wasn't a hill; it was a set of three hills, so it might have been more appropriately named Snodgrass Ridge, but maybe that doesn't sound as good. General Thomas established a line that was approximately one mile long along the Snodgrass Ridges. Longstreet's wing assaulted Thomas' position at Snodgrass Hill around 25 times. In the early phases of the assault, the men of the 39th were still in the tree line procuring ammunition.

Johnson ordered Coleman's brigade to support Fulton's brigade for an assault on the right of Thomas' line. Fulton occupied the spur of Snodgrass Hill, which overlooked the Vittetoe house. To the front was the brigade of Colonel John Mitchell. Mitchell's brigade arrived late on Sunday afternoon, so as they went into line on Snodgrass Hill, they were fresh. Mitchell's brigade consisted of the 78th Illinois and the 98th, 113th, and 12th First Ohio. The 12First Ohio occupied the very farthest point on the Union right. To the left of Mitchell's brigade were the men of General Walter Whitaker's brigade, which included the 96th and 115th Illinois, the 84th Indiana, the 22nd Michigan, and the 40th and 80th Ohio. These were the men that the men of the 39th attacked.

While the 39th was in the rear of Fulton's and Sugg's brigade, the two brigades were having a lot of difficulty in holding off an advance by Mitchell's brigade. Johnson ordered Coleman's men forward. Coleman crossed over the left of Fulton and charged across a small incline in their front, which put them looming over the enemy until they into the ravine amongst them. Again, the men found themselves in a desperate hand-to-hand struggle. When your rifle fires three rounds a minute, and you're surrounded by a jumble of men, bayonets, fists, and the rifle itself are the quickest means of survival. Coleman, in his report, stated that "we charged over the hill upon the enemy, and after a protracted and obstinate resistance (a brigade on our right and Manigault's brigade on the ridge to our left advancing on parallel lines to us), the enemy was completely driven from the position. During the assault, Manigault's mostly Alabama brigade got bogged down, which created a gap between Coleman and Manigault that led to Coleman being hit hard on the left flank of the brigade. The 39th was on the far right, with the men of the First Arkansas mounted rifles bearing the brunt of this miscue.

As darkness fell, Thomas' men withdrew, and Snodgrass ridge was captured and in Confederate control. The point where the men of the 39th broke through at Sunset is memorialized by a monument on Snodgrass ridge. The Confederate army of Tennessee knew they were victorious, and the night was filled with a shrill "rebel yell" down the entire Confederate line. With Thomas' men in a full sprint toward Chattanooga and Rosecrans already in Chattanooga with his other two Corps Commanders, the victory was still criticized. Though Bragg had driven the enemy thoroughly, he hadn't blocked them from Chattanooga, and as Thomas ran, Bragg didn't pursue. The Union forces in Chattanooga had plenty of time to start preparing for Bragg. You would think that after a major victory, things would have been at least moderately cheerful among the Confederate higher command, but they weren't. Following the victory at Chickamauga, there was yet another outcry to relieve Bragg. The Bragg opposition was now joined by General Longstreet.

I'm sure Longstreet wasn't very fond of Bragg, but it also probably didn't help Bragg any that Longstreet was in search of an independent command. The Battle of Chickamauga only adds to the Longstreet argument. I'm not saying Longstreet didn't like General Lee, but Longstreet aspired to be more than just Lee's replacement for Stonewall Jackson. The West was Longstreet's chance to strike out on his own. Following the Battle of Chickamauga, Longstreet probably felt pretty good about himself. In July 1863, Longstreet had to launch an assault on the 3rd Day of Gettysburg ordered by Lee that he didn't agree with. The charge, as we all know, was an absolute disaster. Longstreet supporters will argue that Longstreet did everything he could to stop Lee from murdering his army, whereas Lee will say that Longstreet's attitude ensured the failure of the charge.

In Chickamauga, not under the thumb of Lee, Longstreet launched arguably the most effective charge of the entire American Civil War. Was this necessitated by a major folly by General Rosecrans? Absolutely! But isn't that how war goes? General Lee got a great deal of help at Chancellorsville by Hooker making a ton of mistakes. Chancellorsville is by many considered the Peak of General Lee, but Union General Joseph Hooker might have been Lee's second-best General at Gettysburg; I can't possibly detract from the superhuman efforts of General Stonewall Jackson. That is itself might be a good argument for Longstreet at Chickamauga; he did it without a Stonewall Jackson.

Chapter 19

Another piece of the history of Longstreet's separate assaults at both high-water marks of the Confederacy is the Macon County, North Carolina connection. When Longstreet was assaulted at Gettysburg, Macon County's Company H of the 16th North Carolina was there. When Longstreet's Grand Column assaulted the Union Right at Chickamauga, Companies B and I of the 39th North Carolina were there. The story of Company H is for another day; this day is for the Maconians of Companies B and I of the 39th North Carolina.

When the 39th North Carolina went arrived at Chickamauga, they had 247 men ready for battle. Of that 247, 10 men were killed, 90 were wounded, and three were missing. The regiment suffered 41.70% casualties. Chickamauga was the second bloodiest battle of the American Civil War. When the fighting was over, the Union had suffered 16,170 casualties, and the Confederates had suffered 18,454 for a total of 34,624 casualties out of 125,000 men present. That's a casualty percentage of 27.70%. The men of the 39th suffered casualties at a rate 1.51x worse than all men engaged in the second Bloodiest Battle of the war. The casualty percentage at Gettysburg was 28.48%. The men of the 39th suffered a higher percentage of casualties than the casualty percentage of both bloodiest battles of the Civil War.

As you read through the various exploits of the 39th North Carolina at Chickamauga, it can be hard to keep up with all they did. Every major movement of McNair's brigade involved the 39th North Carolina, and by the time the battle was over, the men of McNair's brigade came to be known as "The Star brigade of Chickamauga." During the battle, McNair's brigade captured ten cannons, several caissons, six ordnance wagons, six wagons of ammunition, 800 rifles, 26 Artillery Horses, and two Separate Union Battle Flags. One of the two was not remembered, but the one that Coleman remembers was that of the 8th Kansas. The 8th Kansas was one of the regiments in Heg's brigade, which meant that the 39th more than likely captured it during Saturday's Battle. The men were allowed to imprint another inverted cannon to signify their second capture of Federal Artillery in battle.

The 8th Kansas had a nine-man detail responsible for guarding their regimental flag at Chickamauga. Of the nine men, four were killed, three wounded, and the other two made it without a scratch. The 39th was pressed harder than it ever had been at Chickamauga. Like at Murfreesboro, they were a Bastard regiment. Alone as North Carolinians in a brigade full of Arkansas troops. For three days, the men of the 39th forged an incredible history with McNair's brigade; they never served in battle with McNair's brigade again. At the high point of the Confederacy in the West, the men of the 39th also had what I would assume was the most memorable weekend of their life in the bloodiest battle ever fought in the History of every American State with, of course, the exception of Pennsylvania. There were more casualties at Chickamauga than there were in the Entire Mexican American War, where so many of Chickamauga's Leaders had earned their first combat experience.

I don't think it's possible for us to imagine what the devastation looked like. The men that were there saw parts of the ground that were literally covered in bodies. The ground was black from sporadic brush fires caused by the various fiery components of a battle. The dirt was literally saturated in blood in places. When a bullet penetrates a man, it carries with it his bone, flesh, innards, and whatever it clings to and hurls it wherever it lands. As men's arms and legs were blown off and their torsos cut in half, their bodies would travel the path of least resistance until it met the ground or another advancing Confederate.

As artillery tore through ranks, a cannonball would rip through a kneecap, grapeshot would pepper a man or a group of men with multiple wounds, and canister shots left heaps of men. When we watch a movie about the Civil War, no one can possibly recreate such a macabre scene. It's beyond comprehension. My meager attempt at even trying to describe the violence doesn't begin to do the carnage justice. Somehow men like the men of the 39th saw all this destruction and kept moving forward to meet the same fate. The men that didn't die were left with the never-ending memory of those that did. Macon County was there, and Macon County fought hard. Of the 10 Killed in the 39th North Carolina, six were from Macon County. Five of them were from Company I. Of the 90 Wounded, 22 of them were from Macon County, and two of those ended up dying later. Macon County had 29 casualties of the 103 suffered by the 39th North Carolina. Nearly 1/3 of the regimental Losses were Macon County men. My Grandfather Joseph Beasley was commended for gallantry for his actions in The Battle of Chickamauga.

Macon County's Chickamauga Losses

Company B (one killed, two died of wounds, eleven wounded, and one captured)

Company B Percentage of 39th North Carolina casualties: 14.56%

Company B (killed)

Pvt. John H. Allen (wounded 19th September, died of wounds)

Pvt. John Henry (wounded, died of wounds)

Pvt. Thomas H. Lowe (killed 19th September)

Company B (Wounded and Captured)

Third Lt. William A. Holbrook (wounded in the left thigh, 19th September.)

Cpl. William J. Bates (wounded in the hip, 19th September)

Pvt. James L. Black (wounded 19th September)

Pvt. Thomas W. Glaze (wounded 19th September, later killed in the Atlanta Campaign)

Pvt. Pinkney Lomax (captured)

Pvt. John R. Love (wounded 19th September)

Pvt. James M. McGaha (wounded 19th September)

Pvt. Peter C. Mason (wounded)

Pvt. Joseph Melton (wounded)

Pvt. Ephraim Tallent (wounded/skull fractured 20th September)

Pvt. Joseph M. Thompson (wounded)

Pvt. William A. Thompson (wounded 19th September)

Company I (five Killed, nine wounded)

Company I Percentage of 39th North Carolina casualties: 13.59%

Company I (killed)

Sgt. Silas M. Dean (killed 20th September)

Pvt. James A. Cross (killed 20th September)

Pvt. James A. Glidewell (killed 19th September)

Pvt. James Jacobs (killed 19th September)

Company I (Wounded.)

First. Sgt. George A. Campbell (wounded 19th September. Also wounded later at Spanish Fort)

Sgt. John A. Baldwin (wounded 19th September)

Cpl. James T. Winstead (wounded 19th September)

Pvt. Levi Buckner (wounded 19th September)

Pvt. Felix A. Dowdle. (wounded)

Pvt. John J. Frady (wounded, returned to duty 28th September)

Pvt. Elijah Gribble (wounded 19th September, captured later during Atlanta Campaign, then captured again at Spanish Fort)

Pvt. Charles Haney (wounded in both thighs 19th September, killed later at Spanish Fort)

Pvt. Franklin H. Hastings (wounded 19th September)

Act V

Post-Chickamauga, Florida, and The Atlanta Campaign

21 September 1863-4 October 1864

Chapter 20

Following Chickamauga, the 39th moved along with McNair's brigade and Johnson's Division back to Mississippi. McNair's brigade was then reassigned to the Division of General Samuel Gibbs French. French was a Northern Born Confederate General that was born in New Jersey. French was a West Point graduate from the class of 1843, which also graduated General Ulysses Grant. French served during the Mexican war and was wounded in two separate battles…Monterrey and Buena Vista. French resigned his commission and became a planter in Mississippi. His first wife, Matilda Roberts, was a Mississippian, and they had two children. She birthed him one daughter, and she died along with her second child in childbirth prior to the war.

Colonel Coleman had taken charge of the entire brigade when General McNair fell wounded at Chickamauga, but when the 39th made it back to Mississippi, command of the brigade was given to General Alexander Reynolds, the father of Lt. Col. Reynolds. Reynolds and his father had an interesting post-war story. When the war was over, they, along with other former Confederate Officers, took commissions in the Egyptian army and waged another war against Ethiopia. That's a story for another book.

In whatever amount of time after Chickamauga, it took them 39th to find their way to Meridian; that's where they went into camp until 5 December 1863 when they were moved to Brandon, Mississippi. The 39th stayed went into camp at Brandon with the intention of Brandon being their winter camp. The only major news to report during this time was that General Braxton Bragg, despite his victory at Chickamauga, was replaced by General Joseph Johnston on 16th December 1863.

In January of 1864, Captain Bell wrote his wife about Private Nineveh C. Norris, who had deserted on 18th September 1863 and hadn't returned. Bell also referred to Daniel Guy, who had deserted the hospital at Knoxville on 15th March 1863. Captain Bell was apparently in contact with the home guards back in Macon County and intended for them to capture them both. That was about the apex of excitement at the beginning of 1864.

French's division stayed at Brandon through all of December and January, and early in February, French was ordered to move back toward the old battlefield at Jackson to oppose two corps of Sherman's army. French's men occupied Jackson on the morning of 5th February 1864, and word came that Sherman's Two Corps were inbound. French realized that he was heavily outnumbered to the tune of about 8 to 1. Sherman occupied Jackson that same evening, and French was headed to Mobile, Alabama, where they arrived on 9th February 1864. French's men were bracing for an attack on Mobile that proved to be false. Sherman was headed for Meridian, Mississippi, which he took on 14th February 1864. While at Mobile, Captain Bell states the regiment was subjected to shelling but not any pitched combat.

Captain Bell was arrested on 21st March 1864 and forced to turn in his sword to the adjutant. He was charged with neglect of duty assigned to him by General Pillow in Western North Carolina and for staying in North Carolina longer than he was allowed. This arrest sidelined Bell for the Atlanta campaign, and based on his recollections of being in the rear; he probably preferred it that way. Bell visited the men of his Company B on the front lines, but he was always happy to vacate the front lines after his visits. In his letters home, Bell constantly ridiculed Colonel Coleman, and according to him, Coleman was arrested and court-martialed around the same time for "drunkenness." I haven't found any records of this, but Bell writes it as fact.

The 39th was then ordered away from Mobile and then ordered to Pensacola, Florida, along the yellow river to brace for another "imminent" attack. The Federal attack never came, and for whatever reason, by some divine act of God, the 39th didn't receive any follow-on orders. For more than two months, the 39th was left in Pensacola. Except for having to pull guard, the 39th had an impromptu vacation from the war. They were able to enjoy the much warmer climate for the last stint leading up to spring.

When the men arrived in Florida, they took up a campsite on a little plateau that overlooked the Yellow River. The campsite was beautiful to look at, but it had a serious issue with rattlesnakes. The men killed more than a dozen the evening they arrived, and Coleman instructed them to set a large fire around the entire perimeter of the camp and to kill every one of the rattlesnakes within the border. The ground was covered in pine logs, and so at least one rattlesnake was able to evade the Confederate authorities.

First Lt. John Davidson and Captain Samuel Mount were in the same tent that night and woke the following morning to a small rattlesnake that had crawled under their blankets. When Davidson and Mount woke up, I'm sure that was quite a scene as they slowly reconciled their morning thoughts with the reality of venomous snake in easy striking distance. The men quickly killed the serpent, but one can only imagine how quickly or methodically they must have sprung up from their sleeping. The camp came to be affectionately known as Camp Rattlesnake.

The area around their camp was very remote, with a very small population. Given their incredibly remote and cut-off location, the 39th kept up a very strong picket line at all times. I'm sure to the men the whole arrangement must have felt too good to be true. They were in a lush forest, tons of wildlife, and much quieter than the fields of Murfreesboro,

Jackson, and Chickamauga. They had to be wondering when it would all come crashing down.

The men were given instructions to shoot anything that moved after dark without challenging. There was at least one case where Lt. Davidson saved the lives of three men that didn't take the warning very seriously. He challenged some men walking in that had been out foraging instead of firing on them without question. The three men turned out to be members of the 39th that had gotten complacent. If Davidson had followed orders, he would have been without his right to kill them. But he didn't. Davidson recalled this story around 1899, some 35 years after it had taken place, and felt he still had to justify his not following orders.

The area around Camp Rattlesnake was teeming with deer, wild bees, and the river was abounding with fish. The men did not have to starve as they did at other times during the war. They were surrounded by a lush country that was untouched by the pillaging armies of either side. On one occasion, Coleman organized three squads of six men with three very specific missions. Squad 1 was headed up by the Surgeon Dr. Alfred Hatcher and was detailed to catch all the fish they could get, Squad 2 was detailed to bring in as many deer as they could, and Squad 3 was detailed to gather up as much honey as they could.

When the day was over, Squad 1 came in with loads of fish, and a second trip was needed to get a large turtle that

Dr. Hatcher had caught. Squad two came in toting three large bucks. Squad 3 marched back with each man carrying a large bucket of honey. The bounty was divided up, and a large feast was prepared. The large turtle was handed over to the cooks, and the 39th enjoyed turtle stew the following day.

Chapter 21

About 1 May 1864, orders came for the 39th to cook three days rations. That was a command that was very telling in the Confederate Army. When the order came for three days' rations, something was about to happen. Around 1700 on 1 May 1864, the 39th had to bid farewell to its home away from home at Camp Rattlesnake. The men of the 39th were sad to leave as their time in Florida was the most peaceful. It was like being back home only without the Mountains. The men were marched 40 miles North to Pollard, Alabama, where they loaded up on trains and arrived at Resaca, Georgia, on 8 May 1864.

Johnston consolidated his army at Resaca, and the 39th took up a position on the extreme left of the Confederate Line at Resaca and began digging in on a bluff that overlooked the Oostanaula River. Skirmishing at Resaca began on Friday the 13th. The 39th was positioned to guard/support a nearby battery. Union artillery observed the location of the battery and opened fire. The Union Artillery was of little consequence, and most of the rounds whizzed over the top of their position. The area where they impacted killed several artillery horses in a hollow behind the bluff.

Heavy skirmishing and exchanges of artillery were the extent of the hostilities of that Friday. On Saturday morning, Sherman coordinated a full-scale assault along the entire four-mile Confederate Line, which was largely unfruitful.

General Schofield's Army of Ohio made an attack on the Confederate Center to no avail. This assault was managed very poorly, owing in part to the Commander of his 2nd Division being drunk. The Division Commander General Henry Judah was relieved of command soon after the battle. Judah was on his last chance after having been previously disciplined for alcoholism. His last chance cost the lives of every man that was slaughtered due to his mismanagement of the field.

Johnston answered with a counterattack on the Union Left. The 39th was part of this counterattack around 1600 on 14 May 1864. The 39th had dug a trench line on the bluff and put up a brush fence along the top of it. The men were given the order to charge, and they climbed over the brush fence and onto the field to commence the charge. The first three men over the fence were the flag bearer, Bryson of Company K, Sergeant Corbin of Company I, and Lt. Davidson of Company C. There were multiple Bryson's in Company, so I'm not sure which one it was, Corbin wasn't a Sergeant that I'm aware of, and he wasn't in Company I; he was in Company B. Perhaps he was transferred, and it wasn't recorded. Either way, a Jackson Man, a Macon Man, and a Cherokee Man were the first to bound over the brush fence.

On the other side of the fence, Bryson stood tall and yelled for the men bounding over to rally on the colors. No sooner had he muttered the word, a cannonball ripped his arm off, and Sergeant Corbin was knocked to the ground from the concussion. Lt. Davidson was still standing but was shell-shocked and unable to move. The dropped flag was quickly picked up by James Wesley Shelton, who carried the flag for the rest of the war. The regiment dressed on the colors quickly and began rushing toward the Union Left. The men moved forward across the field very rapidly, and just before they entered the timber, the men were ordered to lie down and catch their breath.

The men laid in the prone and were looking forward through the tree line and into the fields beyond where the field was strewn with both Union and Confederate corpses, the earth being blown open, shards of flesh, bone, fat, and pools of blood in every direction. Company I was in advance of the regiment as Skirmish Line but in the rear of an Alabama Regiment. As the Alabama Regiment was pushing forward, its ranks were being torn to shreds, and their heavy casualties had caused them to slow their movement, which had held up Crawford's Skirmish Line. The main body of the regiment caught up with Crawford's Skirmish line, by which time the charge had been halted with such heavy casualties, the main body, along with the Skirmish Line, and the Alabama Regiment formed a line against the Union defenders. The fighting raged well into nightfall to a point where the lines could only be traced by muzzle flashes.

The stubbornness to retire after dark was that both forces were contending for the possession of a hill west of town. As twilight faded to complete darkness, the 39th, along with the rest of the Confederates, pulled back to their trenches from where they first launched the assault. As the line pulled away, the Union Line erupted with firing. Volleys followed the line all the way back to their trenches, and Lt. Davidson found himself having to take refuge behind a large white oak stump. As the firing died down, a decently sized group of Union men advanced forward with Axes and began chopping down trees and building up breastworks with them. Davidson was so close that he could distinctly hear them talking to each other and carrying on a detailed conversation. Lt. Davidson kept as low to the ground and as quiet as he could. He waited until he could time his retreat with the crashing of a large tree. Davidson bounded back to the trenches as quickly as possible. Luckily, he found the safety of his trench line without being shot or at least being discovered.

Back at the trenches, Davidson came upon a large body of men sharing their latest war stories and heard Colonel Coleman inquire about Davidson's fate. The men recounted to Coleman that Davidson had last been seen when the regiment pulled out, and they were afraid he'd been struck down by one of the final volleys. At that moment, Davidson sprung back into the trenches and proclaimed. "Here I am."

Coleman looked at Davidson like he was looking at Lazarus and asked him, "Lieutenant Davidson, where have you been?" Davidson replied that he had stayed behind to see if the Yankees would take possession of the hill. Coleman replied, "Oh no, they have not." Davidson insisted they had the hill and moved Coleman closer where he could hear the swinging of axes and the logs being drug across the ground to build up defenses. Coleman was convinced and complimented Davidson for his bravery. Davidson recounted years later that a tale of his "bravery" had been recounted to an Atlanta Newspaper. He never knew who told his story to the paper. Davidson joked about his "bravery" himself. That isn't just my commentary. It seems that dropping to the ground, getting cover, and getting as low as he could work out for him. That's solider 101. A little bit of dumb luck made it the story of a war hero.

Chapter 22

On Sunday, the 15th, the battle continued at a lesser scale. The 39th formed a line overwatching the Union's new breastworks that they'd built overnight. Davidson was assigned to cartridge duty. He, along with a small group of men, set up in a cave near the bluff where they rolled cartridges and stuffed bullets through the entire day. The men would put the cartridges into haversacks and sling one over each shoulder. En route to the Confederate Line, they would exit the cave and bound up to a large poplar tree and catch their breath; then they would bound to a spot behind a pine log and then move up to the line to distribute cartridges down the line. The men on the line were firing on the new federal breastworks. Davidson recounted that every time ahead, a hat or hand would emerge that it was instantly targeted by the whole line.

Johnston was concerned with the exposure of his army, and the loss of the high ground on the field, and the fact that Johnston was fighting a defensive campaign. Johnston gave the order to withdraw the Sunday Evening 15 May 1864. Johnston and Confederate President Jeff Davis were not on the same page at that time. Johnston was convinced that if he could tactically outmaneuver Sherman and keep his casualties low, he could draw the war out long enough to make the North grow weary of the war and vote out Lincoln in November. There was a large public outcry for peace in the North, and Johnston intended to exploit that idea. Whether he was right or wrong…history will never know as that wasn't Jeff Davis' goal. Davis wanted Johnston to be aggressive and fight the North hard. This difference in ideology would put Johnston and Davis at odds during the Campaign.

Given that the 39th was on the extreme left, the 39th were the last regiment to leave. Although Resaca was a Confederate Tactical loss, the ground on which the 39th was defended was never yielded to the enemy. The 39th held strong. They didn't break the Union Right, but they also held the Confederate left the entire time. Realizing the confederate army was withdrawing, the Union Army was flinging shells into the retreating Confederate Lines. Colonel Coleman gave the command to break ranks and run. It was every man for himself, and when they got to the bridge by which the army had retreated, they found it on fire in 6 different places but still passable. Shells were landing all around them, bursting overhead, and the army was in full retreat. The men of the 39th ran along the railroad until they finally found themselves out of range of the enemy cannons.

The men were exhausted, having had little sleep over the past few days, and they were breathing heavily from the hard run from the field. Their faces were blackened, their tongues were swollen from biting so many cartridges open over the past few days. Black powder was all over their faces and was streaming down from their lips mixed with spit and sweat. They found themselves near the field hospital and with access to a little creek. The men plunged into the water and drank hard. That must have felt like a little slice of heaven in the middle of hell. This wet plunge helped as they crawled back up onto the banks of the little stream. The men sprawled out and started to collect themselves. Men started combing their tangled hair, beards, and whiskers and scrubbing the grime off their faces.

The men were veterans by that time and were keenly aware of quickly turning off the combat switch. When the fight was over…it was over. They now had a chance to rest. The regiment rejoined the army at Lay's Ferry and then proceeded to Calhoun. At Calhoun, the 39th ran into another North Carolina Regiment…the 60th North Carolina. The 60th contained a lot of Buncombe men, which meant that there were several brief reunions of old friends between the two regiments. The 60th also fought at Chickamauga and suffered greatly. The 39th was considered a small regiment with only 247 men present at Chickamauga. The 60th only fielded 150 and lost 40.00% of them. The 39th had lost 40.49% of what it had engaged, so the losses at Chickamauga for both regiments were nearly identical in terms of percentage.

The reunion, of course, was short-lived as Johnston proceeded to fall back to Adairsville, then Kingston, then Cassville. At Cassville, Johnston held a Council of War and decided that Cassville was where he would make his next stand. Johnston succeeded in tricking Sherman into splitting his command and sent Schofield toward Cassville. This was an impressive feat to trick Sherman, but despite forcing the split, the split wasn't successfully exploited.

Chapter 23

At Cassville, the 39th was engaged on Thursday 19 May 1864, which was just four days after Resaca. The 39th were engaged from Thursday 19 May until Saturday 21 May. The Union dialed in on the position well and drove the Confederates from the ditches and back to Cartersville. Lt. Davidson and Lt. Eagle from one of the Arkansas Regiments were left behind with about 100 men to pounds on the breastworks overnight and make sounds that made it seem like the Confederates were going to defend against another assault.

The men pulled out the following day and were protected by a rearguard of some Cavalry and Artillery. The little detail under Davidson was tired from the actual fight and pretending to build earthworks all night. They staggered along the road as the rearguard would form and fire occasionally, and the artillery would stop and fire a few rounds to keep the front of the enemy in check. The men finally made it to Cartersville across a pontoon bridge over the Etowah River. The men got to eat breakfast and take a break in a little pine thicket before they finally found their Brigade at Cooper's Iron Works.

From Cartersville, the army fell back to Allatoona Pass. Sherman deemed the Confederate position at Allatoona pass too strong and not worth it. Sherman had been moving along the tracks of the western & Atlantic Railroad up until that point; Sherman diverted from the railroad and headed south toward Dalton. If Sherman could get to Dalton, he could press Johnston's left flank.

Meanwhile, the 39th had moved from Cooper's Iron Works to Powder Springs, where they had arrived on 23 May 1864. That day they were ordered to reinforce Cleburne at Dalton. That evening while en route to Dalton, two important events took place. The 39th was halted near New Hope Church and told to begin fortifying. That night they also learned that they were no longer a part of McNair's Brigade. McNair, of course, hadn't led the Brigade since Chickamauga, so it was technically Reynolds' Brigade. The men of the 39th were transferred to Ector's Brigade. Ector's Brigade consisted of the 9th Texas, the 10th Texas Dismounted Cavalry, 14th Texas Dismounted Cavalry, 32nd Texas Dismounted Cavalry, and probably most exciting to the 39th was that the fifth unit of Ector's Brigade was the 29th North Carolina. The men of the 29th were also mountain men. They hailed from seven mountain counties, three of which were the same counties that furnished men to the 39th. Those three counties were Buncombe, Jackson, and Cherokee. Many brothers, cousins, and neighbors were now in the same Brigade.

At New Hope Church, Johnston had predicted what Sherman would do, and when Sherman didn't attack Allatoona Pass, Johnston successfully put his force in the way of Sherman's advance. Johnston also fooled Sherman enough that Sherman thought Johnston had only a tiny force at New Hope Church. Johnston set a good trap when he put his skirmishes out about 3 miles from the mainline at New Hope Church. Sherman dispatched Hooker's Corps to deal with Johnston's small force at New Hope Church.

Joseph Hooker was now a Corps Commander in the west, and as he moved his three divisions on Johnston's Skirmish Line, he was a little over one year removed from his command of the Army of the Potomac. Robert E. Lee and Stonewall Jackson had clashed with Hooker at Chancellorsville and had delivered a dynamic blow that thoroughly defeated Hooker. Hooker was now pushing his Corps through the woods and proceeded to drive the skirmishers in toward the mainline.

On the morning of 25, May 1864 Hooker's Corps began to move across a burning bridge and immediately started taking fire. Sherman didn't believe a large force could have moved into New Hope Church that fast and still believed the force at New Hope Church was tiny. Hooker's Corps was ordered forward and attacked the Confederates at New Hope Church at around 1600 on the evening of 25 May 1864. The Confederates were not a tiny force, and they were deeply entrenched. They had dug in and created log bunkers that dotted the area, which was already built up with downed timber.

General John W. Geary's Division attacked the position at New Hope Church as the spearhead. Geary was the first mayor of San Francisco, California, before the war. Geary advanced on the Confederate position one Brigade at a time, which allowed for each successive Brigade to be torn apart. The Confederates were able to concentrate their fires on the much smaller front of a Brigade as opposed to defending against a huge column.

The Division of General Alpheus Williams lost over 800 men in just a few moments during their assault. The terrain was terrible to advance on as it was full of small hills followed by holes with thick underbrush and little stacks of fallen timber. The defense of New Hope Church was perfectly conducted by the defending force, and the Confederates were able to mass their fires on an enemy front in well-fortified positions with clear fields of fire. The way the Confederate Army conducted itself at New Hope Church could be used to teach modern military doctrine for defense. It was sound. The terrain was very bad for assault, the ground was heavily defended, and the plan was executed well by the Confederates. The Union, with all these odds against them, also poorly coordinated the assault.

All these factors are what led to one Confederate Division being able to check an entire Union Corps. The Union suffered nearly 1700 casualties assaulting New Hope Church. The defending Confederates lost approximately

450. The 39th suffered in the engagement at New Hope Church; three were wounded and one missing. The battle officially took place on 25-26 May 1864 but what immediately followed was more sporadic skirmishing for the next nine days after the battle was technically over. The 39th was under fire sporadically this entire time.

Chapter 24

On 4 June 1864, Johnston withdrew in the direction of the mountains. The 39th left the vicinity of New Hope Church in the dark on a night when the rain was coming down in sheets. The ground had been turned so soft that men were sinking deep into the ground as they walked. Men were sinking into the ground and having to pry their shoes and legs out from the mud. During the movement from New Hope Church, nearly half the regiment lost one shoe or both in the sticky mud. It's interesting to note here that the question of whether the men of the 39th were barefoot at the time was essentially answered. They had shoes to lose.

After June 1864, it's unclear if they ever get issued shoes again. Did they buy their own? One thing we can surmise is that somewhere around half the regiment was walking barefooted across Atlanta for at least the rest of the Atlanta Campaign. Lieutenant Davidson is the man that recorded this piece of history for us. As he and the rest of the regiment were trudging through the deep Georgia mud, Davidson found himself having to walk across a footbridge. As he inched along, he lost his balance and fell into what he basically recounts as a big mud hole. Davidson then gives us a good explanation of what it was like around New Hope Church when he notes that the regiment had been standing in ditches with mud and water up to their knees for the last several days. When Davidson crawled out of the mud hole,

I'm sure he was covered in that Characteristic Red Georgia Mud for the rest of the march.

The march was halted at Lost Mountain, and the men of the 39th were each given a shot of sorghum seed whiskey. I don't know if it was meant to motivate them or help them after the march, but the actual result was that it caused the men to vomit heavily. There were roughly 500 men that were all sick at one time. The men were puking uncontrollably and were unable to help one another as they were all equally miserable. On 8 June 1864, Johnston fell back to a strong position at Kennesaw Mountain but maintained one division at Pine Mountain. Pine Mountain was pushed out toward the Federal Line in advance of Johnston's position at Kennesaw.

On 14 June 1864, three very important men were standing on Pine Mountain. General Sherman himself was conducting a personal recon of the area, and he personally observed some men observing the Union Lines. Sherman gave the command for the artillery to open fire on the position. The order was directed to Major General Oliver Howard, and as the order was given, Sherman rode off to conduct further recon. The order was given to the 5th Indiana Battery to begin firing on the position. The battery commenced firing without knowing how important their target was.

The Confederates under fire were none other than Joseph Johnston and two of his Corps Commanders. The first shot went flying over the heads of the men. Colonel William Dilworth of the 4th Florida was also part of the group, and he yelled for the men to disperse and take cover. Johnston and Hardee were quick to take cover, but Polk was slow to move. History isn't quite sure whether it was the second or third cannonball, but a 3-inch shot tore through Polk's left side and ripped through his body, killing him instantly. The 39th had just lost its Corps Commander. Polk wasn't known as being a Strong Corps Commander, but he seemed to be universally loved by the enlisted men. Lt. Davidson referred to him as their "beloved Corps Commander" in his recounting of the day Polk was killed. Of course, the 39th always had a soft spot for other Tar Heels. Sherman didn't have much to say in his breaking the news to Washington.

"We Killed Bishop Polk yesterday and made good progress today."

On 16 June 1864, the Commanding Officer of the 5th Indiana Battery that gave the order to fire on Polk was killed by a Confederate sniper. This was two days after he gave the order. I have found no reference to what exactly happened with the sniper, but I imagine this was a prescribed, surgical hit. Polk's lifeless body was pulled from the field, and a very elaborate funeral was held for him in Augusta, Georgia, where his body was buried in the sanctuary of the church in Augusta. In 1945 his body was moved to New Orleans, Louisiana, where his body at the time of this writing is still buried in the Sanctuary of Christ Church Cathedral. His body is just to the right of the pulpit. At the time of this writing, Polk's remains are in danger of being moved due to the current controversy of Confederate memorials and statues. As of this writing, Polk is still resting in peace.

The man that took over for Polk was General William Loring. Like Polk, he was a native North Carolinian. Loring, however, had a lot more military experience than Polk, having fought in the Mexican war and had also battled the Comanches, Apache's, and Kiowas in the American frontier. One other major difference is that Loring's final resting place was disturbed in August of 2020 when his remains were dug up from underneath a monument built to honor him. He had been buried at the monument in St. Augustine, Florida, for about 134 years. Without diving too much into politics, we should get back to the story at hand.

Leaving 2021 and journeying back to 17 June 1864 with Loring in charge of the late Leonidas Polk's Corps, we would find ourselves amongst a torrential downpour. The rain was pouring on the soldiers and compounding the movement of both armies. It was difficult for men to traverse the muddy lanes of Georgia during this time, and horses, artillery, and wagons were virtually useless. Men from both sides were pulling wagons out of mud, vainly trying to stay dry, and the overall climate was just miserable for all involved. Sherman himself was writing Washington at the time and complaining of the weather and of how slow Thomas' Army of the Cumberland was. They seemed to want to entrench everywhere they went and to strike camp whenever they stopped. Sherman felt like Thomas' as Commander all the way down to his Privates, were so stuck in defense mode that they couldn't move fast enough to strike the Confederacy as hard as Sherman wanted to.

Chapter 25

The armies were going at each other constantly during this time, and the lines were so close that skirmishing, picket exchanges, and behind enemy lines recon were constant. The same day Polk had died, our famed regimental historian Lt. Davidson was taken from the 39th for good. Davidson was hospitalized in Georgia hospitals for the next few months, which included Atlanta, Macon, Augusta, and Columbia. When Davidson recovered, he was put on light duty at the hospital at Salisbury, North Carolina as a clerk under Dr. Joel Hall. Being on the front lines ended for Davidson, but it wasn't near over for the rest of the men of the 39th.

On 18 June 1864, the 39th formed a very exposed line near the Latimer Farm. About ¾ of a mile from the Confederate position was Federal artillery which was shelling the position constantly. In coordination with the Artillery barrage, General Thomas pushed three divisions toward the Confederate position. Thomas' 3 Division succeeded in pushing the Confederate Skirmish Line back to join the rest of the position inside the trenches. The Union was able to push forward and occupy another trench that was immediate to the front of the Confederate Line. Johnston knew the chances of being overran were very high and yet again pulled his forces out and pulled them back to Kennesaw Mountain. In action at Latimer Farm, the 39th had six men killed, eight wounded, and one missing. Among the wounded was Lieutenant William T. West of Company B. Lt. West was wounded in the head and died a few days later. West had been captured at Murfreesboro and nominated for the Badge of Distinction for the same battle.

On 27 June 1864, Sherman launched a frontal assault on the Confederate force at Kennesaw Mountain. Sherman was repulsed with heavy casualties in one of the few victories for the Confederacy during the Atlanta Campaign. The 39th was said to have had played very little part in the battle as they occupied a position away from the main battle line.

From Kennesaw, Johnston moved to a prepared position at Smyrna, and on 4 July 1864, the men of the 39th as part of Loring's Corps occupied the right of the Confederate Line. That day Loring's Corps received the Brunt of the Federal Attack at Smyrna. The men of the 39th and the rest of the Corps held the line and the Federals, like one week earlier, were unable to break the Confederate Line. Despite repelling the Federal advance, Sherman still outmaneuvered Johnston and again forced Johnston's Army to retire to a new position along the Chattahoochee River which they occupied on 5 July 1864. On 5 July 1864, I had a 4th Great Grandfather and Great Uncle that were captured. Although there was no combat on 5 July 1864, I can only imagine that they might have been captured on Picket Duty. My 4th Great Grandfather Joseph Manson Beasley and Uncle Charles Beasley were first moved to Louisville, Kentucky, and then imprisoned at Camp Douglas, Chicago, Illinois. Charles arrived on 20 July 1864, and Joseph arrived on 28 July 1864.

On 7 July 1864, William W. Loring relinquished command of Polk's former Corps to General Alexander P. Stewart. As of 7 July, the 39th belonged to Ector's Brigade of French's Division of Stewart's Corps. Stewart was a Tennessee Native, West Point Class of 1842, in which he graduated 12/56, and after a brief stint in the army, resigned to become a Professor of Mathematics at Cumberland University and later the University of Nashville.

By 8 July 1864, Sherman was fording the Chattahoochee upstream from the Confederate position, and Johnston again withdrew this time to Peachtree Creek, which put him dangerously close to the one Prize that Jefferson Davis didn't want to lose. The Confederate Line was now just 4 miles away from Atlanta, and Sherman didn't show any sign of slowing down. Johnston formed a line at Peachtree Creek that had the 39th and Stewart's Corps on the Confederate left.

With Sherman pounding on the doors of Atlanta, Jefferson Davis was already on the cusp of removing Johnston from command. Johnston sent correspondence to Davis in Mid-July which urged action to be taken regarding the Union Prisoners at Andersonville Prison camp. This cryptic message was all Jeff Davis needed to see. The writing was on the wall that Johnston was making plans to abandon Atlanta to Sherman. Johnston and Davis did not have the same ideas about how to defend the Confederacy that Summer. Johnston, despite his skillful movements and his strategy aimed at reducing the number of Confederate casualties, Davis viewed these actions as indecisive and not aggressive enough. Davis replaced Johnston as Commander on 17 July 1864 and replaced him with General John Bell Hood.

Hood was certainly aggressive, and his aggressiveness was abundantly clear when you first met him. He had to strap onto his horse. Hood had lost the use of his left arm from a shell wound at Gettysburg, and the reason he had to be strapped into his horse was because of his fake right leg, which had been amputated about 4 inches below the hip due to being struck by a minie ball at Chickamauga. Hood didn't let only having one arm and one leg get him down. Hood had an orderly that followed close behind him with his crutches. I've just got to say here that even though Hood was considered reckless, what a damn badass, right!? He had every excuse in the world to go home and stay home. Instead, his tenacious attitude and never say quit mentality had a one-armed, one-legged man in charge of the Confederate Army of West. Some might call a man like that foolish; I can't help but be impressed.

Chapter 26

I'm certain Hood would have reacted the same way even if he hadn't been under immense pressure to act. On 19th July 1864, heavy skirmishing broke out between the Armies again. During the skirmishing of the 19th, Macon County's Sergeant William Tippett was killed. Tippett wrote to Captain Bell about the regiment's actions at Chickamauga while Bell was away from the regiment. Tippet also shows up in one of Bell's letters. Bell mentions that Tippett had been shot in the head and killed, Jovan J. Jones was wounded in the right knee, Milton Rhodes received a flesh wound in his right arm, and Andrew Jackson Moore was wounded on the 21st bad enough that the bullet broke the bone in his right shoulder. On the morning of 20th July 1864, the Union Army of the Cumberland began crossing Peachtree Creek and immediately took up defensive positions. Hooker's Corps took up position on the left of the Union Line, and One Single Division of 4th Corps under General John Newton occupied the right. The rest of the 4th Corps had moved east of Atlanta.

The Union Line was actively digging in and in the process of constructing earthworks when they were hit by Hood's first assault since taking charge of the army of Tennessee. Hardee's Corp struck them on the right, and Stewart's Corps struck them on the left. Cockrell's Missourians and Walthall's Mississippians struck first on the left with Ector's Brigade in support. Hardee's Corps encountered heavy resistance without making much headway on the right. The attack by Stewart's Corps on the left went much better. The 39th took part as part of the assault on the left, drove two Union Brigades, captured four pieces of artillery, and captured a large portion of the 33rd New Jersey and their battle flag.

The Union launched a successful counterattack and, greatly aided by well-placed artillery on the Confederate Line, succeeded in thwarting Stewart's attack and pushing the Confederate Line back to their breastworks. The attack was extremely costly in a very short amount of time in a very small space. The Confederates suffered around 2500 casualties, with the Union suffering around 19:00. Hood's first major assault was poorly coordinated and extremely costly. Hood was not off to a good start after the disaster at Peachtree Creek. In the actions at Peachtree Creek on 19-20th July 1864, the 39th had 15 more men killed, wounded, and captured.

Then in a move that was all too familiar for the Atlanta Campaign, Hood fell back and occupied the City of Atlanta. Heavy fighting broke out east of Atlanta on 22nd July 1864, and on 27th July 1864, Ector's Brigade was moved to the left of the Confederate Line at Atlanta. The following day, Ector's men were moved again; this time to reinforce Walthall's Mississippians at Ezra Church around two miles west of Atlanta. Walthall was already heavily engaged when the 39th and Ector's Brigade arrived and took up a position on the extreme left flank.

Hood launched another desperate attack which sustained around 3000 more casualties while only inflicting about 600 on the Union. In the fighting at Ezra Church, the 39th was heavily engaged, and among the wounded was General Ector, the Brigade Commander, and General Stewart, the Corps Commander. General Ector's wound led to the amputation of his left leg at about the knee. Ector didn't recover in time to ever take another active field command. With the wounding of Ector, Colonel William H. Young of the 9th Texas took control of the brigade.

As July ended, Hood had launched three highly costly offensives outside of the city to stop Sherman from entering the city. During August, Hood was relatively stagnant besides constant maneuvering on one another. Sherman also commenced a campaign of constantly shelling Confederate positions and the city of Atlanta itself. Ector/Young's Brigade rotated on Picket Duty in front of the defensive works west of the city.

In one of Bell's letters on 27th July 1864, he notes that the men of the regiment, himself not included, were laying in ditches but weren't currently engaged. He notes that they were under constant shelling. Bell also referenced the poor food situation in Georgia at the time despite being harvest time. The men were getting to eat a few potatoes, collard greens, mill, and bread. Bell mentioned that corn was starting to come in. Bell also references that his wife should get a man by the name of Baldwin to make her some dog skin "as dog skin makes nice shoes." Bell during this time was in the rear instead of the front lines, and command of the company was with 1st Lt. William T. Anderson. Anderson had been wounded in the shoulder and groin at Murfreesboro. Bell didn't seem to have much interest in going back to the front.

During August, Hood was relatively stagnant besides constant maneuvering on one another. Sherman also commenced a campaign of constantly shelling Confederate positions and the city of Atlanta itself. Ector/Young's Brigade rotated on Picket Duty in front of the defensive works west of the city.

Bell described how the men were when he made a visit to the front line. They were generally well but dissatisfied with the lack of food. They wore out from having to pull so much duty and being in within sight of the Yankee breastworks; they were constantly on the alert and tucked behind cover. Bell stated that the Pickets were engaged constantly but had suffered surprisingly few casualties. Wilburn A. Collins had been wounded in his left middle finger, and his hand had to be amputated. Also, Bell references that James Thaddeus Nichols was wounded on the right side of his face by a shell. Bell mentioned that several others were wounded but not anyone his wife would know. Bell wrote his wife that on his trip to the line, some 40-50 rounds had impacted within 100 yards of him, and he'd been admittedly so scared he returned to the cooking train. Bell was sympathetic to the women and children that had been killed in the constant shelling. Bell felt sorry for the remaining women and children in Atlanta but didn't understand why they didn't just leave. Bell also noted that a new house was being burned down daily. Bell's letter at the same time references that Private John Wood Owen of Company B had gone home. I haven't found any record of wounding or sickness, but it doesn't say he deserted either.

Chapter 27

On 23rd August 1864, Captain Bell wrote his wife again to relay more news of the regiment's actions in defense of Atlanta. Around 1000 on the morning of 20th August 1864, Thomas Glaze of Macon County's Company B was shot through the head on the Picket Line. The ball struck his army and passed through his body. He was killed instantly. One of Buncombe's Company D Corporal Lot Whitaker was killed on picket the same night that Glaze was, and Dennis Tippet of Macon's Company B was wounded slightly in the head, and an unnamed member of Jackson's Company K was wounded slightly in the arm.

The Picket Line suffered at least four casualties in one day, and Bell personally observed the mortal wounding of two men from a shell while he was visiting the front line. There were soldiers and civilians dying every day in Atlanta, and Bell was surprised the casualties weren't worse than Sherman as the shelling never stopped day or night. Bell further confided in his wife his already negative view of Sherman's tactics. He questioned if it would be different if Sherman were seeing it up close rather than shelling from so far away or if Sherman enjoyed shelling women and children.

On 26th August 1864, Sherman's army made a new and powerful thrust which severed two of the railroads leading into Atlanta. The 39th, along with the remainder of Stewart's

Corps, were left behind to defend Atlanta as Hood moved the Corps of Hardee and Stephen Lee to attack the Union near Jonesboro. Hood waged a disastrous two-day battle in which two of Hardee's Brigades were effectively destroyed. The two Corps then moved to Lovejoy's Station and were joined by the 39th and the rest of Stewart's Corps as Hood officially abandoned Atlanta on 1st September 1864. The 39th and the rest of French's Division were detailed as the rearguard for the retreat of the Army and went into line on 3rd September 1864 at Lovejoy's Station.

The abandonment of Atlanta brought the Atlanta Campaign to a close. Johnston had been relieved of his perceived intentions of abandoning Atlanta. Hood abandoned Atlanta anyway. I would argue that Hood's relieving Johnston didn't accomplish anything other than higher casualties. During the Atlanta Campaign, the 39th had seen its Brigade and Corps Commander wounded and had endured roughly four months of constant combat. Atlanta wasn't one large battle; it was a series of constant battles that elapsed over a greater period. There were more Casualties during the Atlanta Campaign than the Battle of Gettysburg. In total, both sides suffered around 67,000 casualties. At Gettysburg, both sides suffered around 51,000 casualties. There is just a large difference between three days of fighting and four months of fighting.

When you think of the Battle of Gettysburg as a campaign, you can more greatly appreciate the extreme loss of men during the Atlanta Campaign. Instead of names like Devil's Den, Wheatfield, and Peach Orchard, think of New Hope Church, Latimer Farm, and Peachtree Creek. I'm not sure what would be worse. You had the choice of three days of absolute genocide or four months of slow murder. Neither option was a good one, and I only put it in this context to shine a light on the suffering of the army of Tennessee that is so often overlooked. The men of the 39th, by the time it was said and done, had 16 killed, 57 wounded, and 15 missing, totaling 88 casualties. This was close to their 103 casualties sustained at Chickamauga. This again was a string of casualties absorbed over three days vs. four months. Which is worse? The men of the 39th had suffered 191 casualties in those two engagements. In two engagements, the company lost nearly two companies worth of men. Between Chickamauga and the Campaign for Atlanta, the 39th lost nearly 20% of its full fighting force. I'm sure many homes had silent, tearful supper tables, and countless sermons in little valley churches made memorials of the men lost in the Atlanta Campaign. The Maconians had lost many within their two companies and had certainly done their part in a futile struggle to defend Atlanta.

After the capture of Atlanta, the forces on both sides laid low for a while and tried to figure out what the other was doing. Sherman, of course, was happy that he had driven a wedge through the very heart of the Confederacy and now was in firm possession of Atlanta…the heart of the Confederate War Machine. Both armies seemed to just be catching their breath. As already mentioned, the ranks had a lot of newly formed shortages, and the men of both sides were exhausted. Hood became convinced that Sherman was no longer on the offensive and decided to launch his own. Hood wanted to take back Tennessee and felt that retaking Tennessee would be far more important to Confederate Morale than a dozen victories in Virginia.

On 21st September 1864, Hood moved his forces to Palmetto. Hood sent Stewart's Corps in the direction of the federal garrisons at Acworth and Big Shanty, which were successfully captured on 4th October 1864. The men of Stewart's Corps began ripping up sections of the railroad and succeeded in destroying around 8 miles worth of track. Stewart then received ordered to move toward Allatoona Pass and capture the small garrison there and fill the railroad pass with debris to render it impassible. Stewart assigned French's division to take Allatoona. As French moved his Division toward Allatoona, the majority of the 39th were detailed to act as security for Confederate Artillery. In addition to securing the artillery, a detail of approximately 40 members of the 39th joined French's Division in the assault on Allatoona. As French marched toward Allatoona, the Atlanta Campaign ended; and the Tennessee Campaign officially began.

Act VI

The Tennessee Campaign and Spanish Fort

5th October 1864-11th May 1865

Chapter 28

French's division was dispatched to attack Allatoona Pass at the request of General Hood. The Allatoona Pass was a section of railroad that went through a pass that was cut deeply into the ground. The Federals were heavily entrenched in two separate redoubts and were under the command of General John Murray Corse. Corse had attended West Point for two years and opted out of Military service in pursuit of practicing law. He was a Pittsburg, Pennsylvania native but moved at a young age to Iowa. His father served six tours as mayor of Burlington, Iowa.

Corse started his military career as Major of the 6th Iowa and built an impressive career as both a Staff Officer and Field Officer. Corse had fought at Corinth, Vicksburg, and was wounded at Missionary Ridge. Corse was sent along with 21:00 men to secure the pass, and his mission was to hold the Allatoona Pass and prevent Hood from severing Union Lines of communication. Corse didn't have a large force to defend with, but most of his men were armed with Henry Repeating Rifles. The Henry's could fire around 28 rounds per minute which were even faster than the 14-20 rounds per minute of the Spencer Repeating Rifle. One soldier armed with a Henry could fire as many rounds as a little over nine men armed with muskets.

The battle opened on the morning of 5th October 1864 at around 07:00 when French began shelling the pass with approximately 12 cannons. Corse answered with about half as many guns when his 12th Wisconsin began firing back. The artillery duel lasted until about 09:00 when French sent a demand for Corse to surrender.

French attacked the Western Star Fort in force and sustained the attack for over two hours. French's command crushed two lines of defense leading up to the star fort, and it seemed inevitable that the Corse would be dislodged from the main fortification. Reinforcements came from the Eastern Star Fort, which prevented it, along with a false report that a much larger reinforcement was near. French called off the attack and withdrew at around 14:00. French's withdrawal was extremely premature as zero reinforcements arrived until the following morning.

The fighting in the lines leading up to the star fort was very hotly contested. As the Confederates hopped into their trenches, the battle turned into a brawl. The men of both sides were reduced to fighting with their bayonets and fists. Officers were firing their revolvers off at close range, and the engagement was so desperate that men were throwing rocks and sticks at one another. When the combat gets that close and personal, there is no time to reload and fire again. The fight in an instant like that turned barbaric. Whatever was close at hand, and whatever could be used on the enemy the quickest, became the new armament.

Corse, in my opinion, is best known in his military career for the stand he and his men made at Allatoona. Sherman famously messaged Corse to "Hold on; I am coming!" These words were later pinned into a ballad that commemorated Corse and his strong stand against overwhelming odds. Corse lost a cheekbone and an ear during the fighting, but it didn't end his field service. Corse had sustained casualties to about 27% of his defending force and had inflicted around 35% casualties on the attacking Confederates. The battle was a small engagement, but the violence was astonishing. Of all men engaged, around 30% were casualties. The casualty percentage at Gettysburg was around 28%. This fighting took place over the course of around 2-5 hours. We know that Macon County was part of the 40-man attacking force as Elisha L Kimsey of Macon County was wounded there in his right shoulder.

French had to leave without capturing the pass, blocking the passage with debris, and sustained heavy casualties with numerical superiority and created a Union Folk Legend. Perhaps the worst defeat of all was that he was unable to score the one million rations that were stored there. French's men and the army of Tennessee were in desperate need of rations and, with bad intel, lost that opportunity. We can look back now with all the information at hand and know all the things that the French didn't know at the time. With the protection of his men after a costly battle that was preceded by a devastating campaign, it's easy to understand why French called off the assault.

Along with a host of other casualties, the Brigade Commander was among the wounded. General William Hugh Young took the spot of General Ector when Ector was wounded at Ezra Church. General Young had his horse shot out from under him, then he himself was wounded in the left ankle, which led to the amputation of his foot and to his being captured. General Young had one hell of a war. He had two horses shot out from under him at Murfreesboro, and he was wounded in the right shoulder, wounded in the right thigh at Jackson, shot on the left side of his chest at Chickamauga, neck, and jaw at Kennesaw, and now he had been wounded in the left foot. General Young had been wounded six times! General Young was carried from the field that day and was carried to the rear. Unfortunately, the ambulance that was transferring him was captured by Federal Cavalry the following day. With the wounding of General Young, Colonel Coleman of the 39th took command of the entire brigade formerly known as Ector's and then Young's Brigade.

As Coleman took command of the brigade, the Confederacy was preparing for one last great campaign…the Campaign for Tennessee. Hood wanted Tennessee back very badly, and Hood was a tough brawler that was prepared to do anything to take back Tennessee. Hood moved west of

Rome on 10th October 1864. Sherman moved toward Rome soon after and poised General George H. Thomas to defend the Tennessee River in preparation for a perceived crossing by Hood. Hood went away from Rome and headed back toward Northeast Georgia toward Resaca, and on 13th October 1864 captured the garrison at Dalton, Georgia. Hood then proceeded to tear up 20 miles of track between Resaca and Tunnel Hill. On 22nd October 1864, Hood proceeded to Tuscumbia, Alabama, and started refitting/resupplying his Army. Sherman let Hood march into Tennessee unopposed. He felt confident that Hood's invasion could be handled by General George H. Thomas. Sherman himself prepared the rest of his Army to depart Atlanta and head for Savannah in his infamous "March to the Sea." As Hood went north, Sherman confidently headed further south. The Tennessee Campaign would officially be set for Hood vs. Thomas.

Chapter 29

On 2nd November 1864, Hood's army of Tennessee began crossing the Tennessee River. Hood encountered bad weather and flash flooding as he tried to cross, and this slowed his crossing significantly. The crossing ended up taking Hood's Army for nearly three weeks. Hood then moved his Army toward Columbia and intended to seize bridges across the Duck River and cut off the command of General John M. Schofield from the rest of the Army.

Hood's men encountered horrible weather on their march to Spring Hill. The men marched through rain, sleet, and snow. The campaign was already delayed, and any element of surprise was gone, but the horrible weather only slowed the campaign down further. Forrest's Cavalry was having human difficulty, but the campaign weather coupled with major supply issues, the campaign was having a great deal of effect on Forrest's horses. When Forrest got to Spring Hill, Schofield was already waiting for him. The Army didn't catch Schofield by surprise whatsoever. Despite how prepared they were, Hood came very close to cutting Schofield off. Hood blamed General Cheatham more than anyone because he felt his orders to attack were not carried out on time and that when they were, Cheatham only mounted a puny attack which allowed for Schofield to make his escape.

Whatever the case, Schofield slid his force to Franklin, Tennessee. Franklin had pre-existing entrenchments that the Union Army quickly commenced to improve. The Union Army set up a defensive line from the northwest to southeast of town. Hood attacked the Union Army at Franklin in a devastating frontal assault which led to over 6,000 casualties. The Union Line suffered around 2,000 casualties and repulsed the Confederates. Luckily, the 39th was detailed to guard the army's pontoon train during the battle and thus missed the fighting at Franklin. There were six Confederate Generals killed, seven wounded, and one captured. There were 55 regimental commanders that were killed, wounded, or captured. The results were devastating to the army of Tennessee.

General Schofield, after absolutely slaughtering the army of Tennessee, withdrew toward Nashville and reunited with General George H. Thomas. Hood did not stop his campaign, and he continued his pursuit of General Schofield. When Hood arrived, he formed his Army in the hills of Southern Nashville and began entrenching and throwing up defenses. At the time, General French was on a leave of absence, and his division was attached to the division of General Edward Walthall. Walthall was a Virginian and, like so many leaders in the army of Tennessee, had been banged up severely. Walthall had been wounded three times already and most recently at Franklin.

Coleman's brigade was originally intended to be on the left in support of the Cavalry, but just before the battle, they were moved and put in the reserve of Walthall's Line. The Confederate Line at Nashville consisted of somewhere between 22,000 and 30,000 men. On the Union Line were approximately 55,000 men. In the best-case scenario, Hood was outnumbered around two to one. Hood knew he couldn't trust his men into certain death again, and Hood was extremely low on high-level leadership. Franklin had cost him so many, and most notably, Generals Cleburne and States Rights Gist were among the dead. If Thomas didn't attack, it's unclear what Hood would have done.

Hood's Line occupied fortifications that were about four miles long. From right to left was the Corps of Benjamin F. Cheatham, followed by the Corps of Stephen D. Lee, followed by the Corps of Alexander P. Stewart, and on the farthest left was Cavalry under James R. Chalmers. The left of the line also held five redoubts with 2-4 guns and around 150 men apiece. Hood proceeded to send three brigades of Infantry to strike the railroad between Nashville and Murfreesboro and attack the Federal garrison at Murfreesboro. A few days later, he sent two more brigades of Infantry and two brigades of Cavalry also toward Murfreesboro. The entire column sent to Murfreesboro was put under the command of Nathan Bedford Forrest.

Hood apparently thought this would draw Thomas out of his fortifications in Nashville. It did not draw him out until he was ready, the units he sent to Murfreesboro were driven back, and his force at Nashville was even more outnumbered. The X-Factor in the whole scenario is that Forrest, his strongest commander, along with Forrest's Dynamic Cavalry, was out of the fight. The men of the 39th were serving in the Brigade of their own David Coleman, Walthall's Division, of General Alexander P. Stewart's Corps.

On the other side, General George H. Thomas was under a lot of pressure. Hood was smashed at Franklin, but his presence in Nashville was still a threat. Thomas knew he had to attack. President Lincoln was growing frustrated with what he perceived as procrastination, and Grant was already frustrated with Sherman having marched to the sea and leaving the north open to a possible invasion from Hood. A very bitter ice storm hit Nashville on 8th December 1864 and continued with sub-freezing temperatures until around 13th December 1864 when Grant had sent General John Logan to take over command from General Thomas. Grant himself left Petersburg on 14th December 1864 in order to personally take command but only made it as far as Washington. When he received word that the battle had begun, Grant turned around and put his focus back on General Robert E. Lee.

Chapter 30

On 15th December 1864, Thomas launched a massive attack on the Confederate left under General Stewart, which included the men of the 39th. Coleman's brigade was moved to defend the Hillsboro pike. Stewart's Corps consisting of around 5000 men, was hit by 45,000 men, and as all the redoubts on the left of the Confederate Line collapsed, the men of the Coleman's Brigade were completely cut off from the rest of Stewart's Corps. Coleman's brigade was very small and was in danger of being captured.

During the night, Coleman's Brigade was relieved and moved to a point near the Granny White Pike as Hood had fallen back and established a new defensive line. Thomas didn't allow the Confederates to rest, and on 16th December 1864, he smashed his army into them again against the Corps of General Benjamin F. Cheatham. Cheatham's Corps had been moved overnight to the Confederate left to support the greatly decimated Confederate left from the previous attack on the 15th. General Cheatham's Division was hit hard and scattered in disarray. Coleman's brigade was moved to the Confederate left to counterattack and met heavy resistance again. Coleman's brigade was already tiny and now was further stressed by the losses from the first day's fight. Despite being badly torn up, the 39th, with the help of another brigade, was able to halt the Federal advance.

The other brigade was a brigade of Daniel H. Reynolds' Arkansas Brigade. Among Reynolds' Brigade were the men that had fought alongside the 39th at Chickamauga. Particularly among Reynolds' Brigade were the men of the 25th Arkansas that had made the charge with the 39th on 19th September 1863, which went the farthest on the 1st major day of fighting at Chickamauga. These reliable veterans held the line against incredible odds but were unable to take back the Granny White Pike that Cheatham's men had abandoned. It wasn't long until Stewart's Corps began to fall back as well. The men of the 39th held until the bitter end of Nashville, but their retreat was aided by a strong rearguard action by the Corps of Stephen D. Lee and the good fortune of bad weather in the Nashville area greatly slowing down the movements of Thomas' Army. Lee's Corps played heavily in the ability of the Army to escape, but enough can't be said about the stand of Coleman's and Reynolds' Corps, which allowed the safe passage of the army of Tennessee.

As we look back on the history of the 39th, it's important to understand that in the minds of most of the men of the 39th, Nashville was their first defeat. In the realm of history, we consider some of the army of Tennessee's escapades as known defeats. In the mind of many, the army of Tennessee soldiers, a lot of the withdrawals of the army of Tennessee were tactical and intentional. In recollections of veterans of the 39th, Nashville was considered the first defeat of the 39th, and they attribute the defeat to the fact that they were fighting General Thomas which was a southern-born General, the absence of their General Johnston, and the fact that they were fighting "true western men." The men of the 39th generally felt that western fighters were the superior Union fighting force. 1st Lieutenant Cathey, in his post-war recollections, affirmed this fact and went so far as ranking the types of Union Men they met on the field. He considered the "western men" as the strongest, followed by the foreign-born Union men, then the middle states, and by far the worst were considered to be the "Down-Easters." This is what Lt. Cathey attributed as the reason for the "first defeat."

Whatever the reason, the 39th was defeated, Stewart's Corps was defeated, and the army of Tennessee was defeated. At Nashville, the army of Tennessee took another 6,000 casualties, which was double the loss of Thomas' Union Army. Hood retreated with approximately 16 to 24,000 of the original army of 45,000 he had brought. At best, Hood had about 53% of his command left; at worst, Hood had about 36% of his force remaining. Whichever number you choose, Hood had led his army to decimation. The army of Tennessee as a fighting force was incapacitated. The results of the Tennessee campaign were horrendous. Hood was a brawler and an absolute badass, but I don't think there's any possible way to paint Hood's campaign in a positive light. Hood's aggressiveness had destroyed the army of Tennessee.

Johnston's tactics in Atlanta weren't flashy or productive in the eyes of Jefferson Davis, but the enormous loss of life would have never happened under General Johnston. Hood's aggressiveness had netted the Confederacy, a whole load of nothing. The Army wasn't an Army. As it retreated from Nashville, it was a Corps at best. The men that Hood had sacrificed couldn't be replaced. The men that were captured could not be replaced, and the war for the army of Tennessee truly ended in Nashville. The men would go on to mount various defensive operations, but as an offensive unit with true initiative, the army of Tennessee was done.

Hood's Army began recrossing the Tennessee River near Florence, Alabama, on 26th December 1864. The 39th served with Forrest's Cavalry as the Confederate rearguard, and at Sugar Creek, Tennessee, on the same day, the lead elements of the Army were crossing, engaged the enemy one last time to defend the retreat of Hood's Army. On 28th December 1864, the 39th was the last Confederate unit to cross the Tennessee River. The Army moved first to Tuscumbia, Alabama, then they moved to Iuka, Mississippi, then to Corinth, and finally settled in Tupelo, Mississippi, where he went into camp on 10th January 1865.

Chapter 31

From Tupelo, Coleman's Brigade was then ordered to Mobile, Alabama, to support the garrison commanded by General Dabney H. Maury. Maury was a Virginian that had been an instructor at West Point, author of several military training books, and had nearly lost his arm in the Battle of Cerro Gordo during the Mexican war. Maury also fought the Indians in wars in the Oregon Territory and Texas Frontier.

The men of the 39th were assigned to the garrison at Spanish Fort, Alabama, and were part of the larger spectrum of forces that were designed to defend Mobile Bay as part of the Department of the Gulf. The other Confederates were assigned to Fort Blakely about five miles north of Spanish Fort. At Spanish Fort, the Confederate Garrison consisted of around 2500 men. Coleman's brigade was placed on the Confederate left and was supported by a small Confederate Gunboat.

On 27th March 1865, Spanish Fort came under attack from General Edward Richard Sprigg Canby's force of 30,000-man force. The men at Spanish Fort were outmanned 12 to 1. Canby was a native of Kentucky and veteran of the 2nd Seminole War, Mexican War, Utah War, and the New Mexican War with the Navajo. Canby had also seen service in New York and California with the U.S. Army. Canby had a wealth of military experience before the Civil War began. Canby was also wounded aboard the U.S.S. Cricket by a guerilla in Arkansas in November of 1864. After the Civil War, Canby again served with the U.S. Army in the Modoc War, where he was shot in the head twice and had his throat cut by members of the Modoc Tribe during Peace Negotiations in Northern California. Canby was the only General to be killed during the Modoc War.

Canby, despite having extreme numerical superiority, opted against a full-on front assault on Spanish Fort. Canby opted to dig trenches that faced the fort and build additional rifle pits to close the distance between his forces and the small Confederate garrison. Confederate sharpshooters and artillery harassed Union Engineers and Sappers as they worked, but Canby also had a force of his own sharpshooters and his own artillery, which he used to support his forward units.

By 8th April 1865, the Sappers had moved the line to a position immediately in front of the Confederate Line. Canby proceeded to bombard the fort with his 90 guns. The Confederate Garrison had only around 30 guns to answer this harassment. Around 17:00, the 8th Iowa attacked through on the Confederate left. Just after dark, the Union Army broke the Confederate left. What was left of the 39th constituted many of the casualties and captured. Given confusion on the field and the darkness, the Union Army fell back to its attacking position. The garrison had sustained around 744 casualties which were around 30% of its total strength. Under darkness's cover, the remainder of the garrison followed a little footbridge across the river and escaped to Fort Blakely and Mobile.

On 9th April 1865, General Lee surrendered his army of Northern Virginia to General U.S. Grant. At the same time, Canby's force occupied an empty Spanish Fort. Canby waited until the morning had allowed the Confederate force to escape. What he allowed to escape amounted to around 17:00 men at best. That same day Canby's forces captured Fort Blakely, inflicting another approximately 3,000 casualties on the Fort Blakely Garrison. With the fall of Spanish Fort and Fort Blakely, Mobile was soon to follow. On 12th April 1865, Mobile was officially captured by Union forces three days after Lee's Surrender and three days before the assassination of Abraham Lincoln.

President Lincoln and General Grant were both scheduled to attend Ford's Theatre on 14th April 1865, but General Grant opted to visit his children in New Jersey just prior. At around 22:15, John Wilkes Booth crept into Lincoln's theatre box and fired a fatal round into the back of Lincoln's head. Booth was a Confederate Spy from Maryland and had intended to kill both Lincoln and Grant. After a momentary scuffle with Major Henry Rathbone, but Booth stabbed him and escaped. Lincoln went into a roughly 8-hour coma and died across the street at the Petersen House around 07:22 on the morning of 15th April 1865.

With the fall of Mobile, Maury and his command fell back to Meridian, Mississippi. A small fraction of the 39th made it to Meridian with him. During the defense of mobile, the men of Macon County's Company B numbered around 20 in Company B, and 29 in Company I. This meant that between both companies, they were at around 18% of original strength. In the battle of Spanish Fort, Company B had one killed and 11 captured, and Company I suffered one killed, two wounded, and nine captured.

On 4th May 1865 at Citronelle, Alabama, General Richard Taylor surrendered his Department to General Canby, and by 11th May 1865, the Army was paroled at Meridian, Mississippi. The surrender came about a month after the Surrender of Lee's Army. The men of the 39th were surrendered, and their war was over. Macon County's Companies surrendered around 25 men. Company B, led by 1st Lt. William T. Anderson, surrendered himself and seven others. Company I was led by Captain James G. Crawford, who surrendered himself and 16 others. Collectively at the time of surrender, 9% of the two Companies remained. Among them were my 4th Great Grandfather Andrew Stiles and his brother William Stiles. Andrew isn't recorded as being wounded or being captured during the war from 25th March 1862 on his enlistment day until he was Paroled on 11th May 1865. Apparently, Andrew brought his little brother back with him from furlough while the regiment was encamped in Florida. His little brother William was wounded in his right arm at Atlanta.

The preservation of the flag of the 39th was per regimental historians affirmed by concealing it on the person of Lt. Robert H. Brown of Company K. Brown took the flag and hid it on himself around the time of the surrender. Brown took it all the way home with him, and the flag was displayed for years after when the 39th came together for reunions after the war. With Lee surrendered, Johnston's Surrender on 26th April 1865, and the final major surrender of Taylor's men in the far west, the war was over. The men of the 39th and soldiers all over the Confederacy began their march home. Besides the men who surrendered in Alabama, the 39th had prisoners all over the northern states.

Rank	Name	Company
Pvt.	James L. Black	B
Pvt.	William W. Cabe	B
Pvt.	W.D. Fulcher	B
Pvt.	Robert A. Hall	B
Cpl.	James Sidney Slagle	B
Pvt.	James S. Thomas	B
Pvt.	Washington G. Thomas	B
Pvt.	Isaac A. Waldrup	B
Pvt.	George W. Cabe	I
Pvt.	John L. Cabe	I
Pvt.	Wilburn A. Collins	I
Sgt.	Joshua A. Franks	I
Pvt.	John C. Fulcher	I
Pvt.	Franklin H. Hastings	I
Pvt.	Albert Alphonse Mashburn	I
Pvt.	John G. Mashburn	I
Pvt.	John R. Mashburn	I
Pvt.	William J. Mason	I
Pvt.	James A. Odom	I
Pvt.	Humphrey P. Pendergrass	I
Pvt.	John A. Pendergrass	I
Pvt.	John W. Scroggs	I
Pvt.	Andrew J. Stiles	I
Pvt.	William H. Stiles	I
Pvt.	A.N. Upchurch	I

Credits

The men of the 39th North Carolina who truly wrote this history.

North Carolina Troops:1861-1865 Volume X Infantry 38th-39th,42nd-44th regiments. Compiled by Weymouth T. Jordan Jr. Unit Histories by Louis H. Manarin.

www.carolana.com

The Civil War In North Carolina: Soldiers' and Civilians' Letters and Diaries, 1861-1865. Volume II: The Mountains. Edited by Christopher M. Watford.

The Macon County, NC Historical Museum. Especially George Shook in providing me various documents and research information on the 39th North Carolina.

Chickamauga and Chattanooga National Military Park.

Captain Alfred W. Bell Family.

Davidson Family of Cherokee County.

Lieutenant Benjamin Cathy Family.

Men of the 39th at the end of the war found themselves surrendered, or in prison, out west fighting in the U.S. Army, and in many cases hiding out in the mountains to avoid conscription. Whatever the case, the men that stood in Franklin to be enlisted in October of 1861 and March of 1862 found themselves in much different circumstances in April of 1865. After 1285 days of war those that weren't dead were changed forever. They have been in the ground for more than 150 years and are buried all over Macon County,

North Carolina, surrounding counties and states, and at least as far west as Colorado. Physically they are buried but I resolve not to allow their legacies to be buried for theirs is a cautionary tale. In the middle of Franklin in First Methodist Cemetery and in its cemetery lie both Captains of the Macon Companies. My grandfather lies in Rush Cemetery and the other lies in an old family cemetery in the middle of the woods alongside the old wagon trail in the Hickory Knoll Community of Macon County. Their names are remembered 15 decades later...Joseph Beasley and Andrew Stiles may their names and the men of the 39th North Carolina be remembered for another 15 decades.

www.ingramcontent.com/pod-product-compliance
Ingram Content Group UK Ltd.
Pitfield, Milton Keynes, MK11 3LW, UK
UKHW020424250726
13967UKWH00007B/2799

9 781915 206756